The Seventh Jar

Advance Praise for *The Seventh Jar*

'A brilliant physics student from St Stephen's College, a top-ranking MBA graduate from IIM Ahmedabad and a highly regarded PhD from Columbia Business School, Prof. Srikumar Rao uses his vast intellect and deep experience to provide us a solution to turn our lives from one of fear, hatred, anxiety, jealousy, uncertainty, dissatisfaction and unhappiness to one of positivity, happiness, inner peace and energy. Srikumar has taught at many of the world's top business schools and generations of students have found his course to be life-changing. He shows us how we generate "mental models" to create our own "realities" that bring negativity to us and to those around us. He provides us with a well-researched and proven methodology to create new models and new "realities" to make our lives more peaceful, happier, purposeful and better. In these days of unmitigated mental stress arising from our complex relationships with work, family, friends, love and self-perception, Prof. Rao's proven methodology is a boon to every person on this planet for attaining mental peace, happiness and energy. I have personally benefited from what he shares. This book is a must-read for every one of us'

N.R. Narayana Murthy,
founder and chairman emeritus, Infosys

'*The Seventh Jar* is a transformative guide that bridges the wisdom of ancient spiritual teachings with modern management practices. By distilling timeless practices into practical exercises, Rao empowers individuals not only to aspire to their highest goals but to achieve them with a sense of inner peace and purpose. This book is more than a guide to success – it's a roadmap to living a life of meaning, joy and balance, all while cultivating the deep change needed for lasting impact'

Marshall Goldsmith,
executive coach and author

'In *The Seventh Jar,* Srikumar masterfully guides readers through a transformative journey of self-discovery and empowerment. Each chapter encourages us to question our realities, eliminate stress and embrace a life filled with awareness and creativity. By weaving practical strategies with profound insights, the book illuminates the path to true freedom and happiness, inspiring us to actively create the lives we desire. This compelling read is not just a guide – it's a call to action for anyone seeking to unlock their fullest potential'

M.R. Rangaswami,
founder, Indiaspora

THE SEVENTH JAR

Your Path to Personal Mastery and Success

SRIKUMAR RAO

Foreword by Price Pritchett

BLOOMSBURY
NEW DELHI • LONDON • OXFORD • NEW YORK • SYDNEY

BLOOMSBURY INDIA
Bloomsbury Publishing India Pvt. Ltd
Second Floor, LSC Building No. 4, DDA Complex, Pocket C – 6 & 7,
Vasant Kunj, New Delhi, 110070

BLOOMSBURY, BLOOMSBURY INDIA and the Diana logo
are trademarks of Bloomsbury Publishing Plc

First published in India 2025
This edition published 2025

ISBN: PB: 978-93-61310-31-7; eBook: 978-93-61312-30-4
2 4 6 8 10 9 7 5 3 1

For sale in the Indian subcontinent only

Typeset in Fournier MT Std by Manipal Technologies Limited
Printed and bound in India by Gopsons Papers Pvt. Ltd., Noida

FSC www.fsc.org MIX Paper | Supporting responsible forestry FSC® C191020

To find out more about our authors and books visit www.bloomsbury.com and sign up for our newsletters

To all sentient beings who long for complete freedom and lasting happiness. This is only available when the web of the great illusion is torn apart and realisation dawns that there is only One. There are no others.

Contents

Foreword

My dear friend Srikumar Rao has a gift. He's exceptionally good at helping you pause and see the subtle flaws in your mental habits and use those insights to transform your life. His wisdom sneaks up on you through gentle reasoning as he poses questions and tells stories.

The Seventh Jar is conversational and easy to read, but Srikumar makes you think differently. In today's world filled with quick fixes and superficial solutions, his lessons have gravitas and ring true like those of a sage.

At the heart of his teaching is mastery – not mastery over others but mastery over the self. In a world that pulls us in so many different directions, personal mastery allows us to gain control over two things that matter the most: how we choose to *perceive* and *respond* to the world around us. The book shows you how to cultivate that mastery, not as a one-time effort but as a lifelong practice.

I'm impressed by the practicality of Srikumar's approach. He first asks you to reconsider your common take on reality, then he offers straightforward techniques for how to live more consciously. Srikumar asks you to focus on the 'emotional tenor' of your thought processes and the power of your beliefs or 'mental models'.

This is not a book of abstract philosophies. It's a manual for action. The practices will reshape how you size up your world, break through your limiting beliefs and help create the life you desire. The work this demands of you might push you out of your comfort zone, but that's where true growth happens.

The Seventh Jar delivers fresh, powerful coaching for those who are willing to engage in the core work of transformation. It's not about adopting shallow strategies or applying the latest trendy techniques. It's about simple but profound shifts in the way you handle the things that happen in your life. Your new viewpoints and actions can unlock a level of self-management that can take you far beyond mere success.

As you dive into these pages, understand that you're not just learning new concepts. You're beginning a transformational journey. The journey will require effort and introspection. It will challenge your assumptions about what's possible. And the book will be a game changer for those who are ready to embrace it fully.

I encourage you to take Srikumar's lessons seriously and apply them to your life.

This is your invitation to operate from a new angle of creative thinking that can bring personal mastery. Trust me, you'll be rewarded with a far richer level of living.

Price Pritchett

Consultant and bestselling author

1

Are You Living Your Ideal Life?

Have you ever felt dissatisfied and unhappy with the circumstances of your life? Consider this vision – you wake up in the morning, suffused with an ineffable feeling of joy. Your blood sings at the thought of being who you are and doing what you do. As you go through the day, you feel like falling to your knees involuntarily in gratitude for your good fortune, the good fortune that has been bestowed on you. Does this sound like your life right now? Most of you are probably not even close, but I would like to tell you that this life can be yours. A life such as I just described is your birthright. All you have to do is reach out and claim it.

I am Professor Srikumar Rao and more than two decades ago as part of my own quest for an ideal life I realised the value of the teachings of the great masters – from the Buddha to Ramana Maharshi. I taught a course called The Seventh Jar: Your Path to Personal Mastery and Success, which combined my spiritual learnings with management practice. I taught this course at some of the top business schools in the world – Columbia Business School, London Business School, Kellogg School of Management at Northwestern University, Imperial College London and the Haas School of Business at University of California, Berkeley. I have helped thousands of participants and executives take the first step on their individual quest – the quest for happiness, the quest for a perfect life. In this book I'm going to share some of what I have learned and perfected over the years. This will be the first step on a journey you will take, a journey that will last for the rest of your life.

When I was a doctoral student at Columbia Business School I found it difficult to find fulfilment in my own dissertation. I quit for a while and worked in corporate America. For a long time I could have sworn that the world consisted of two sets of people, those who passionately hated their jobs and those who merely disliked them, and I was very busy shuttling from one to the other. It was not a very happy place to be. There was one semester when it simply got to be too much. I was in academia at the time, and I basically taught my courses and ruminated over what an ideal job should be. All my life I had been reading books, spiritual biographies, mystical autobiographies, and these took me to a different place, a very calm place. And then I would get back into the hurly-burly of life, and that calmness would vanish. I instinctively knew that this was not right. I didn't have a separate personal life and a professional life. I had one life and either it worked, or it didn't. So, when I put together the syllabus for the course, I was doing it primarily for myself. I was working to improve my life.

I offered it for the first time at Long Island University in 1994, and it did well. I moved it to Columbia Business School in 1999, and it simply exploded. It became the only business school course that had a university-wide draw. I had dozens, hundreds of students apply from Business School, from law school, from Teachers College. I had PhD candidates and administrators take the course and many of them reported that their life had changed profoundly. Subsequently word got around, and the course moved to London Business School, then to Haas and other universities. Major corporations too realised that it could be valuable to them and their employees. Now it has grown into a movement that has helped thousands of executives, professionals and entrepreneurs all over the world.

Here is my vision for you. You wake up in the morning with your blood singing at the thought of being who you are and doing what you do. You are radiantly alive every minute of every day. Monday morning is every bit as exciting as Friday evening. Not more exciting because that would make you a workaholic. Not less exciting because that would make you a clock watcher waiting for weekends and vacations. Just as exciting because that means that you enjoy both work and outside activities to the fullest. Your life should be, can be, like that. You can have a completely fulfilling work life and a completely fulfilling personal life and financial security and everything you want. You can have it all.

My students are generally quick to challenge me at this point. The challenges go like this. I want to be the chief executive officer of my company and so does my co-worker. Or I want to be the world champion in chess and so does my playing partner. Only one can make it. So how does this square with what you say?

Bear with me. Each of you *can* fulfil your desire. Your desire to be a chief executive officer or chess champion of the world, but not at the surface level of actually becoming a chief executive officer or chess champion. You have to go one level deeper. Why do you want to be a chief executive officer or the world champion in chess? What does this mean to you? Does it mean financial security? Do you think your mother will be proud of you? Will it make you famous? Go one level deeper still. Why do you want to be famous? Why do you want your mother to be proud of you? Is this what will bring you happiness, a sense of fulfilment? Will it allow you to rid yourself of the demons that are haunting you? It is at this level, this basic level, which drives you to your desire, which in turn drives you to want to be a chief executive officer or chess champion of the world, that you can have everything you want.

Each and every one of you can have everything you want. You may not actually become a chief executive officer or chess champion of the world, but you will be able to get what that represents to you. You will be able to get the sense of fulfilment that all of us are ultimately seeking.

For example, one of my students wanted to join a prestigious consulting firm. He was very bright, deeply driven and felt that this was the best way, in fact, the only way, to have a lasting impact on companies. As I worked with him, he became aware that he did not particularly care for the environment of the firm he was contemplating joining. Soon he changed tracks and became an entrepreneur. He founded a training and coaching firm and his business exploded. He now has more clients than he can handle and is looking for staff. And not by coincidence the programmes that he is conducting are changing the lives of hundreds of individuals. In many cases, he has been hired by companies specifically to engender cultural change, either in a division of the company or in the entire company. He reached his goal much faster than he thought he would and in an entirely different way.

This book is based upon the course The Seventh Jar: Your Path to Personal Mastery and Success and draws from material that I have collected over many decades. Expect that it will completely change your life, your professional life, your personal life, your social life, your spiritual life. It can have such an impact if you sincerely and conscientiously do the exercises which will be shared with you. These exercises work. They work in spades. This is not an egotistical claim. None of the exercises that I'm revealing to you were devised by me. They were created by persons of giant spiritual stature who strode this earth at different times and belonged to different traditions. What I have done is take these exercises, strip them of cultural overtones and cloak them as concepts more fitting for a post-industrial society. They absolutely do work.

As you probably know, profound change in behaviour is not easy to bring about. On occasion, such as New Year's Day or your birthday, you have probably made a resolution or several resolutions. From now on, I'm going to eat healthy, exercise regularly, stop procrastinating and catch up on my backlog of work. Have you? How much success have you had? If you're like most persons, your resolutions fell by the wayside in a few days. Don't beat yourself up about this. Here is something for you to consider. If you try to bring about profound change by an effort of will, you are actually doing violence to yourself. Odds are very good that you will not succeed. But even if you do, it is quite likely that there will be side effects that you're not very happy about.

For example, you want to quit smoking and stop cold turkey. You exercise your willpower. What happens? You stop smoking, but you eat too much and gain weight. Or you decide you have to lose weight and you starve yourself. Another application of will. And you may become thinner, but you also become crotchety and ruin relationships with your spouse and your co-workers. Any time you try to bring about behavioural change through the exercise of will, you're being violent to yourself.

There is a better way. Hundreds of persons have reported deep and lasting change as a result of my programme. This is because you do not use will to affect behavioural change. Instead, you examine your mental models, modify them and adopt different ones. And as you do so, you become a different person. And as you become a different person, your behaviour changes naturally as a by-product. The behaviour change is effortless, though it does require systematic effort on your part to change your mental models. In this book, I will explain how you go about doing this.

At this point you may be asking, is this book for me or is it only for MBA students? Let me ask you. Are you troubled by conflicts in work and personal life? Do you feel that there is something more, something greater that you should be doing with your life? Do you want to leave the world a better place than it was when you entered it? Do you want to find a deeper sense of happiness and freedom? Do you feel that you have great potential and that somehow you're only achieving a fraction of that potential? If you answered yes to any of these questions, this book is for you. If you answered yes to many of these questions, you owe it to yourself to work through this book slowly, carefully and conscientiously.

As you think about your ideal life and why you have not yet achieved it, you will discover that you are actually a prisoner. You are hemmed in by your own thoughts, by the models you have created of how the world works. These lock you in every bit as effectively as any prison cell. Many of us never recognise that we are in prison because we never try the door. It is only when you try the door and find that it is locked that you recognise you are a prisoner. This book is for people who know they are prisoners. What it will give you is a set of tools. There is a lock pick for persons who prefer finesse. There are explosives for persons who would prefer to blast their way out through the walls. There is excavating equipment for persons who would like to dig a tunnel and burrow their way out. There are hacksaws for persons who would like to go at the bars on the windows and many other tools besides. You will experiment with all of these tools. Discover their power for yourself and adapt them to your personality and your needs. And then you will work with them until they are no longer tools, but a part of who you are.

Let me emphasise that. As you work with the exercises in this programme, you will recognise their tremendous power. Keep working with them until they are no longer exercises but have become a part of who you are. When you use them instinctively and all the time is when you will find that the greatest transformation occurs and your life changes dramatically and for the better. Later in this book you will encounter the parable of 'The Seventh Jar'. It shows you how change can happen rapidly in your life and how both success and joy can come flooding in.

Here are some things that will help you get the most out of this book. You must genuinely desire to change and be open to the teachings and tools that I will share with you. I will present you with many different models and ways of viewing the world. Don't judge them. Don't label them good or bad, true or false, or right or wrong. Instead, try them out in your life. And see whether they work better for you in your life than the models that you are currently using. If they work better, adopt them. Modify them to fit your particular circumstances. If they don't work better, simply discard them and move on to the next one. Set aside time to read and engage with the book and the practices recommended. This book is not designed for casual reading. It does require active engagement. It does require conscientious follow-up.

Before you go further to the next chapter, please get yourself a journal. We will be doing several journaling exercises together and I will assign you homework and things to record in and after each chapter. At the start of each chapter, have your journal next to you. Participate fully in the exercises. Really give them your time and your best effort. Pay close attention to your emotional state from day to day, almost from hour to hour. Recognise that this work is a launching point for a journey of self-discovery that will last the rest of your life. It's a really good idea to use this book with other people you trust and who are close to you. If you have a spouse or a friend, have them read the book, do the exercises at the same time, create a support group where you discuss your experiences and meet regularly. Once a month is good. Once a week is even better if you're consistent about it. Think of this as a scientific journey of exploration. You are both the scientist and the laboratory. You might even want to think of it as art. You are the artist. Your life is a work of art and you're shaping and crafting the rest of your life. Ready to begin?

To begin to shape our lives into the ideal life I described, you must first become aware of the emotional tenor or undertones you are currently carrying in your life. Your emotional tenor is the feeling that you derive from your experiences and that you perpetuate in all aspects of your life. It is often the impetus which causes you to act, to react and bring about change. The exercise you are about to learn can be used again and again as a way of helping you take an emotional inventory of your life. This exercise will help shine the light of consciousness on yourself so that you can see clearly and make intentional decisions to bring about your happiness, your ideal life.

You do not need anything special to do this exercise. You can do this exercise right where you are, right in this moment. As we go through this practice, don't judge yourself, just be honest. Don't inhibit the first thoughts that come to your mind. Then take note of these thoughts. In the same way that you might notice a cloud in the sky, just observe without judgement.

Now, begin by taking a few deep breaths and allow yourself to relax. Think of your life as it exists today and in particular your work life. Now bring your attention to your job, the actual work that you are doing, not the people you work with or your salary, but your actual job function. How do you feel about the work that you do? Is it completely satisfying? Every job has something in it that you find good. What elements of satisfaction do you derive from the work you do? It could be the smile on the face of your customer when they receive the goods or services you provide or perhaps the notion that the work you are doing is benefiting large numbers of people all over the world or it could simply be the knowledge that you are contributing your own unique gift to this work – your creativity, attention to detail, or your valuable time and energy. Find at least one aspect of your work that brings you satisfaction. Now note your emotional tenor. The feeling that arises from this satisfaction. Perhaps you feel a sense of joy, peace, excitement, happiness. Allow yourself to connect with this feeling.

If you are like most people, there are at least a few aspects of your job that are unsatisfying. These could be things such as the long hours required to complete your work or the physical or mental stress involved, or even that the work you are doing somehow contributes negatively to the end user. Think about these aspects for a moment now. What elements of your work are unsatisfying, and why do you find them unsatisfying? Once again, note your emotional tenor around these unsatisfying aspects of your work.

Remember, don't judge yourself, just notice it in the same way you might notice a passing cloud in the sky.

Now, let's move on to the people you work with, your co-workers, superiors, subordinates and customers. Relationships are often the most challenging aspects of our lives and can be fraught with conflict and turmoil. By the same token, our relationships with others can bring about serenity and peace. Think of the people in your work life. What aspects of these relationships bring you satisfaction, and who do you find it most satisfying to be with. Note your emotional tenor around these particular relationships. Perhaps they bring you a sense of camaraderie, connectedness and inspiration. Just note these feelings without judgement.

Now think about those parts of your work relationships that are not satisfying, what makes them so and with whom do you have such relationships. Perhaps you have conflicts with co-workers or power struggles with your superiors. Don't become engrossed in the storylines, simply note the emotional tenor that arises from the less-than-satisfying aspects of these relationships. Note any feelings of fear, aversion, aggression. Do this without judgement.

Good, now bring your awareness to the area of intimate relationships. Are you currently in a relationship? Does the presence or lack of a relationship feel satisfying to you? What is it about your current situation that feels good? Perhaps you not only enjoy the aspects of the person you are in a relationship with, but you also enjoy the intimacy and security of being in a relationship or perhaps you enjoy the freedom and solitude you derive from not being in a relationship. Whatever it is, simply note what brings you this satisfaction and note your emotional tenor around it.

What aspects of your current situation are not satisfying to you and why? Perhaps you desperately want to be in a relationship but are not in one or perhaps your current relationship is filled with conflict or is shallow. Do you feel depressed, angry, smothered? Again, simply note your emotional tenor without attachment, without judgement.

Bring your attention to your family life. Your relationship with your parents, siblings, children if you have any. What gives you a sense of contentment? Family relationships often carry a complexity that brings both joy and sorrow. For now, think about the aspects of these relationships that bring you happiness. Perhaps you enjoy a sense of connectedness with your aunt or perhaps a child brings innocent humour back into your life. Think of the positive aspects that arise for you and connect with the feeling tone that comes with them – peace, joy, relaxation, excitement, or whatever it is that comes up.

Now think about the unsatisfying elements of these same family relationships. For many of you, this won't be difficult. Try not to get attached to the drama. Simply note what is not satisfying and connect with the emotional tone around those aspects. Perhaps it brings up feelings of fear, of aggression, confusion and avarice. Don't judge yourself, simply notice.

Now turn your attention to the area of time management. This is often an area which can bring about stress in one's life, a great deal of stress. However, there are satisfying elements to this aspect of life if you look for them. Think about the way you manage your time and find at least some aspect which brings you satisfaction. Perhaps it is the way you plan your mornings before going to work or perhaps you manage your time so efficiently at work that it allows you to work on pet projects. It could even be the way you plan your end-of-the-day activities, so that you have time to spend with your children, on things they enjoy doing or prepare a home-cooked meal. Note the emotional tenor that you feel around this element of your time management.

Now switch your attention to elements about your time management that bring you dissatisfaction. Do you feel overwhelmed? Do you feel as though you're not completing what you set out to do? Simply note this and the emotional feeling tone that is associated with it.

Now that you are becoming adept at noticing the emotional tenor around various aspects of your life, pull back and notice the general feeling, the general emotional tenor of your life. What is the feeling that is most pervasive and that you feel most often? Do you find that you are most often angry, frustrated, depressed or do you most often feel a sense of satisfaction, of joy, of appreciation, of gratitude. Remember, don't judge yourself, just notice, and now bring your attention back to the present moment.

Wonderful! You have just embarked upon the fearless work of witnessing your emotional tenor, just as it is, without judgement. This is a great way to start cultivating awareness so that you can begin to intentionally bring about changes in your life.

This book is all about you and your thoughts and the way in which you create your world. You live in a dream world. You have always been living in a dream world. You have spent your entire life constructing this dream world. You have not been particularly good at this construction, and so you have put in a whole lot of stuff that you don't really like. You moan and groan about this and you make yourself miserable, but you don't accept that you created your dream world and that it is a dream world.

How did you create your dream world? You created it with thought, through your thought patterns. What most of us don't realise is that thought is highly creative. Look around the room that you're in, everything in it, the chair that you're sitting on, the window through which you look outside, the laptop on which you check your email, the automobile that you use. Every single one of these things was at one time a thought in somebody's head. Massive buildings like the World Trade Center, massive tragedies like the felling of the World Trade Center – all of these at one time were a thought in someone's head. Your thought is also creative, endlessly creative. The world that you're living in has been created by your thought. Perhaps you're not happy with some of it or much of it. That is because you have not yet learned to consciously create what you would like to. I will show you how to harness your thought so that it takes you in the direction that you would like to go and helps you manifest that which you would like to see.

I'd like to get started by introducing you to one of the most basic building blocks that you use to create your reality. This is your mental chatter. Your mental chatter is an internal monologue that you have. It begins right from when you open your eyes in the morning, carries on through the day, is with you right now even as you're reading this book. It is with you when you go to bed at night and sometimes it is so loud that it prevents you from going to sleep. It is your constant companion, a companion that you cannot shake loose.

To recognise it, here's how it might go: when you wake up in the morning there is that alarm again. What time is it? I'm sleepy. I don't want to get up. Maybe I can hit the snooze button? Get another 10 minutes of sleep. I need more. Why don't they make snooze buttons that have 30 minutes? What do I have to do today? Oh, gosh, there's that project that's due. I would have finished it last night except Deepak was supposed to send me his part of it, and he never did. How can people be so irresponsible? Let me call him and find out what happened.

Does that sound familiar to you? That's your mental chatter. The wonder is not that you feel tired with this burden that you're carrying every day. The wonder is that you can accomplish anything at all.

Play a thought experiment with me. Suppose there is a new electronic device or computer chip. This is a chip that needs to be embedded in your skull and this chip will give you audio-visual entertainment of the highest quality. Imagine that the surgeon who was going to do the embedding screws up and what you have is a chip that you cannot control. Sometimes the music plays very, very, loudly and sometimes it's inaudible. Sometimes you have glorious pictures and sometimes you have rain falling and falling and grey and dull scenes; in fact, most of the time you have grey and dull scenes. How would you react? How long would it be before you go to a malpractice lawyer and how many zeros do you think would be in the award that you get?

You have such a chip in your head right now and you don't complain. That chip is your mind. It is so much a part of your life that you accept it. You don't question it and that is a mistake. It is a mistake because the mental chatter that you experience is constant every minute of every day from the time you open your eyes to the time you close them at night. That mental chatter is actually shaping your world. Your mental chatter, combined with your mental models, creates your reality. The reality that you experience.

A big part of your mental chatter is your voice of judgement. Where you stick a label on your behaviour and on others. You pass critical comments. Look at her, she's so arrogant. She is constantly criticising other people. You beat yourself up over little thing. Why did I have that slice of pizza, I'm supposed to be on a diet. Why can't I sit down and do my assignments on time? Why can't I be as witty as my friend? Why do I make such stupid comments? You're criticising yourself constantly. You're criticising others constantly, and this voice of judgement could be anywhere from 20 per cent to 60 per cent of your mental chatter.

The rest of your mental chatter could be neutral, but even when you think your mental chatter is neutral, such as when you're planning your day, you will find that you are slipping back into something which is actually negative. You begin by saying, okay, here is what I have to do during the day and as the list grows longer you begin to get a sense of being overwhelmed, so much to do, so little time to do it, will I ever get through it, I am not able to cope, I'm not effective, and you go back into beating yourself up with a negative voice of judgement.

Also notice that your mental chatter carries emotional undertones. Anger, a feeling of being overwhelmed, jealousy, dissatisfaction with the current state of affairs, fear, anxiety, worry, envy. Sometimes your mental chatter can also be strongly positive. It can enter deep peace and serenity. Unfortunately, for most of you, this is a very tiny part of your overall mental chatter. It is unlikely that you are consciously aware of even a tiny fraction of 1 per cent of the chatter that is present in your mind at any given moment. Even when you try to be consciously aware of your mental chatter, you will miss most of it. It's a little bit like throwing a stone at a wasp's nest and trying to count the number of wasps as they come buzzing out. You'll miss most of them. But this mental chatter is enormously important because this is the chatter that is helping shape your life, the reality of your life, the reality that you're experiencing. It is powerful because it comes from your own mind, your conditioning, and it also comes from what you observe in the external world.

The first thing you can do to take advantage of this powerful influence on your reality is to consciously choose what you think about. This is not an easy task. Your mental chatter is going on every moment throughout your busy day, even while you are working on tasks, especially while you are working on tasks. But there are many times throughout your day when you get a span of free time, when the bustle of everyday activity stops momentarily. This could be for a few seconds, such as when you are stopped at a red light. It could be for a few minutes, such as when you miss a train just as you walk into the metro station and have to wait for the next one, or it could be for an hour or more, such as when you have a cancelled appointment. Where does your mind go when you get such time? Odds are that your mental chatter kicks in immediately and you revisit your to-do list and get overwhelmed, or you get distracted by something you have observed or heard or read or you get lost into fantasising about something. What is your underlying emotional tenor as you go wherever you go? Are you anxious, frustrated, hurried, stressed out, angry? Does your voice of judgement begin to take over as you think about persons who wronged you and plot revenge scenarios against them? Do you beat yourself up over your many sins of omission and commission or are you calm and serene, filled with peace, understanding and goodwill, and cheer to the world at large? Are you overflowing with well-being and quietly confident that God is in his heaven and all's right with the world?

I call this place, the place your mind turns to automatically when life's activity stops, your mental screensaver. Your mental screensavers can vary, but you often visit the same place over and over again and more than likely it is not a positive place in which to dwell. Take a moment to reflect on what your mental screensaver is. What is the one thing, or two or three, that always pops up when you are not consciously engaged in something. The good news is that you can consciously choose your mental screensavers and this is a simple but important step that can dramatically affect your reality. Here is an exercise that will help you do so.

As with many of the exercises in this book, this one is best done in a place where you can relax and where you will not be disturbed. If you are not already in such a place, please take a moment to find a comfortable setting where you will not be disturbed. Close your eyes and take a few deep breaths. Feel yourself relaxing. We are going to start by creating a mental screensaver around the area of family. Think back to an event in your life and, in particular, an event involving your family when you were filled with cheer, when joy bubbled up in you and you were thoroughly content; when you were having the time of your life and were of a pleasant disposition. This could be any event, big or small, such as a quiet, intimate Sunday afternoon together, a large family picnic or the birth of a child. As you recall this event, relive it as intensely as you are able to. What about this event brought you such happiness and joy?

Now think about the small details around this happening to help you with the mental experience, to make it stronger. For example, if you are recalling a family picnic, perhaps the weather was beautiful and sunny while your uncle told jokes and sang old Hindi songs. Feel the warm sunlight on your skin, hear the sound of Uncle Ramesh's laughter and relive this event with all of your senses. Most importantly, recall the feeling that this event gave you and connect deeply with it. Allow it to permeate your entire being. Impress this on yourself and your mind as strongly as you can. This is a mental screensaver about your family that you can go back to consciously whenever you have a spare, idle moment. It is especially helpful to go back to the screensaver in moments that you are with your family to help you create even more contentment. It may help to give this screensaver a name such as family picnic.

Now I would like you to clear your mind of this screensaver completely. Let's create a new mental screensaver around your job. Think back to a time in your work life when you were filled with inspiration. When positivity bubbled up in you and you were thoroughly secure and content. When you were filled with goodwill towards everyone around you. This could be any event, big or small, such as a fruitful workday, a creative brainstorming meeting, or a big promotion. As you recall this event, relive it as intensely as you can. What about this event brought you such inspiration and contentment?

Now think about the small details of this event to help the mental experience become stronger. For example, if you are recalling a creative brainstorming session, you might recall the people who were in this meeting. The expressions on their faces, the sounds of the voices filled with creative excitement. You might remember the smell of the markers as idea after idea was captured on the whiteboard. Perhaps you were enjoying a hot cup of coffee during the meeting. Relive the sensation of the warm liquid as you swallowed it. Use all of your senses to recall and reconnect with the details of this event. Most of all connect with the feeling of excitement, inspiration and contentment this moment brought to you. Allow it to become who you are in this moment. Now, give this screensaver a name. You can come back to this screensaver at anytime, especially when you are at work, to help you cultivate feelings of inspiration and goodwill.

Ready to create another one? Let's create a mental screensaver around relationships. Think of someone in your life. Perhaps a spouse, a family member, a close friend. Anyone who causes you to feel that when you are with that person the song that is within you wants to come out. Being with this person inspires you to be who you truly are. Now think of a specific time that you were with this person when you felt an abundance of inspiration, joy and peace. What about this event brought you such inspiration and contentment? Think about the details of this event to help you relive the moment. Perhaps you were enjoying dinner with this person in your home. Recall the sound of music in the background as you laughed and enjoyed playful conversation with this person. Smell the aroma coming from the plates in front of you. Taste the savoury food as you place it in your mouth. Allow all of your senses to relive this enjoyable moment with this person. Now connect with the feeling of being with this person. Let it envelop you in a cloud of contentment. Create a label for this screensaver.

Often when creating screensavers for people it is helpful to use the person's name. You can create a screensaver for every person in your life and use it to reconnect with the positive aspects you enjoy about being with that person. Start practising this with relationships in your life which are fairly positive. As you practise more, try creating screensavers for the more difficult people in your life, people with whom you experience conflict. Focus on moments and aspects about those people that you truly enjoy. Over time you will find the positive elements increasing in those relationships.

Let's create one last screensaver. Think back to a time in your life when you felt a sense of deep peace, when this peace permeated your entire being, physically, emotionally and spiritually. Perhaps it was a time in your life when you were pursuing things that resonated with your heart, such as learning a new hobby, starting a new career, or travelling. Now recall the details around this time in your life. For example, if you were learning to play the guitar, recall the excitement of buying your new guitar, holding it in your hands and hearing the melodic resonance of the strings as you plucked them. Try to connect with as many details of this time in your life as possible. Focus on the feeling tone of this time. How did you feel inside? Perhaps a sense of boundless excitement or maybe an innocent, childlike joy. Whatever the feeling, connect deeply with it and allow it to permeate you right now where you are. This is a screensaver you can use at any time, in any place, to quickly snap you back into the you that you most enjoy being. Give this screensaver a name such as 'me at my best' or 'inspired me' or any name that helps you quickly recall and reconnect with this feeling.

You've done a great job of creating mental screensavers. It's a wonderful way to help you exercise personal mastery over your mental chatter. You may find it helpful to create a half-dozen or so such mental screensavers that encompass different aspects of your life. If you have a favourite restaurant, it probably has several entree choices you love. This works the same way. By creating several different screensavers, you can consciously choose to use one of these in your mental downtime. So have fun with this and enjoy the positive benefits you will begin to receive when you start using these screensavers on a regular basis. You've done wonderfully so far!

2

Deconstructing Your Reality

Let's carry on with our journey.

Your mental chatter feeds into the creation of mental models. A mental model is a notion that you have about how the world works. You have mental models for everything. Together you use your mental chatter and mental models to create your reality.

You have a mental model for how to find a mate. One for how to bring up children. For how to find friendships. For how to get promoted at work.

You have mental models about work and about money – how to get it; how to spend it; how to invest it.

You have mental models about everything. You have dozens of mental models, perhaps hundreds of mental models. Some of your mental models conflict with each other and you may or may not be aware of such conflicts. Somehow you meld all of your mental models into a mishmash and together they constitute the reality that you experience.

The problem is not that you have mental models. Everybody has mental models, and many mental models are actually very useful. I repeat, the problem is not that you have mental models; the problem is that you do not recognise that you have mental models. You don't think of them as mental models. You think of them as reality and the moment you define your mental model as reality, it becomes reality and that is what you start experiencing.

As I said before, many of your mental models are actually very helpful. But quite a few of your mental models are not. They are not serving you well. They are dysfunctional. These mental models are the cause of all the suffering and angst in your life. Here are examples of some mental models that I have come across. Don't laugh as you read them. Odds are very good that you have mental models which are every bit as strange and as dysfunctional.

Here is a mental model of a woman thinking about the world around her:

'I am not important. I am insignificant and this will never change. I won't be rich and famous. No one cares about me. Well, my family cares, but I wish they cared more. My parents haven't come to visit me in a year and a half. My older sister came to visit me, but she only wanted to spend a couple of days with me because she prefers to take a longer vacation in October and go to Egypt. My husband absolutely doesn't care about my problems. All my problems are stupid according to him, but I am expected to lose sleep over his problems. He keeps me awake till 2 a.m. to talk about his midlife crisis or his arguments with his mother. I have no friends in this city. If I don't get a job, I'll have to stay alone at home with my dog as my only companion. My husband is going to work hundred hours a week and he's going to forget about me. My family won't ever come to visit me. I won't make any new friends and my old friends from back home will forget about my existence. My life is going to be miserable I know, and the worst thing is that I don't want to do anything to change that. If I don't get a good job within a year my professional career will be over. I will never have a good job. I won't feel fulfilled, and as we have decided not to have children, I won't have any reason to exist. If I get a good job, I don't know if I will be able to keep it. I have anxiety problems. I can't take stress, I become sick. It happened to me when I worked with my consulting firm and happened again over the summer. I have delicate health. With my health, I will never be able to get a good position. I am not good enough. My life makes no sense. I'm too depressed to continue with this exercise.'

Here is another mental model of a man talking about his relationship:

'My girlfriend has lots of irrational behaviours. She is afraid of crowds, can't go in the metro, can't talk to strangers such as waiters, doesn't like to be kissed on the forehead. She is also insecure and thus unable to accept any help, discuss some topics or share some experiences. I think she's crazy and childish. Things bother her that don't bother me or most people – rain, traffic, workload – and she releases this frustration on me. I want to get away from her because I feel unjustly attacked. She feels alienated because I need space, and she cries. We get into a vicious cycle of fights. I want more space. Maybe I should consider getting out of this relationship.'

And here is a mental model of a woman thinking about how to do well and get promoted at work:

It is really important to look physically good. Wear short heels. They should make you look tall, but not so tall that you are threatening. Shoes should be polished. Hair should be pulled back in a ponytail or bun with no loose strands. Clothes should be conservative but fashionable. A scarf dresses up any outfit. Nails should be manicured, and if you're going to paint them, use only clear or light pink polish. Makeup should not be loud. A little bit of blush and mascara to give you a healthy glow. It is important to take good care of yourself physically. Not being overweight, having bad skin, etc. Jewellery should be subtle but stand out so that you are remembered for the pieces and the stories they are associated with, such as a trip to the Amazon. It is important to act mature. Choose very carefully what personal details you want to share with others. It should never be something that makes others uncomfortable; only stories to unite. When you are out with your work colleagues have no more than three drinks. If you're feeling tipsy, immediately come up with an excuse to leave. Always deliver on what you promise. Don't give excuses if something doesn't work out right. Tell the truth. Nothing can be so bad that you have to lie. Unless you are dying, there are no such things as sick days but remember mental health days are sometimes a matter of life and death if it comes to that. Never ever date in the office. Have a can-do attitude. Don't ever look too busy. If someone talks to you, stop emailing, doing whatever you're doing, give that person your full attention unless, of course, you don't want to talk to them. If you're likely to get some work from your boss, volunteer for it before you are assigned. Volunteer to help others with small tasks. Plug into networks that you can go to when you don't know how to do something. Totally back others, when necessary. Don't backstab. Don't indulge in idle gossip but keep in the information loop. Be visible, but don't play the FaceTime game. Leave when you are done. Take ownership. Become an expert on whatever you are working on. Make projects fun. Think about it as a Martian might. Learn for the sake of the exercise, and it is no longer work. Do special projects that show you are a cut above the rest. Keep your boss and others apprised of what you're doing. You deserve the promotion. Ask for the promotion. Make sure to know all decision makers and make them feel part of your team. Make sure that it is known that you are loyal to the company and the people. Find out what its values are and lift others up with you.'

These are just some examples of mental models. Note how the first two degenerate into a negative, downward spiral. Note how the third has some negative elements but also has many positive elements. What are your mental models like? Where do they take you? Remember, your mental models create your reality. This is actually a very liberating concept. If your mental models create your reality, then you can deconstruct the ones which create a reality that you don't particularly care for. You can then reconstruct them to create a 'better reality'.

Let's take some time out to do a journaling exercise on mental models. Get a pen and your journal and let's begin. Remember what I said before. You are both the scientist and the laboratory. Think of yourself as an objective observer.

Okay. At the top of a clean blank page write four column headings: family, work, love and self. Begin with family. Write the first thing you think of when it comes to your family. Don't stop writing. Don't think. Simply allow your stream of consciousness to pour itself through you and on to the page. Do not judge, do not edit, do not censor. Be completely honest. Let it flow through. You might say under family, 'My husband does not care for me. He's too busy to take me shopping or spend time chatting with me. He spends an inordinate amount of time at work. I wonder whether he is having an affair,' and so on. Be honest.

Let's move to the next column, work. What does work mean to you? Begin with the first thing that comes to mind about work. Write whatever arises for you. Same rules: don't judge, edit or censor. You might say work is so satisfying these days. When I start working, I forget about all the other cares and concerns that I have. I feel a sense of deep fulfilment. Keep going until your thought pattern exhausts itself.

Now we move on to the next column – love. What does love mean to you? When do you experience love for yourself and for others? Is there enough love in your life? Do you give love to others? Whatever is important, set it down. Same rules again, no judgement, no editing, no censoring. Let it all hang out. Remember, you are the only person who will ever read your journal.

And finally, we move to the last column, self. What do you think about yourself? What kind of image about yourself do you hold? Are you by and large happy being who you are or are you deeply dissatisfied with the person that you are, or the person that you think you are? Don't judge your thoughts. Simply allow your hand to translate the thoughts on to the paper as they arise.

What you have just done is taken a glimpse of some of the mental models that you may be carrying around. But this is actually the wedge, the thin edge of the wedge that can destroy one of your most dearly held conceptions. And that conception is the reality of the world that you're living in. Let me explain. People have different mental models. You are already aware of that. Each person perceives the world differently. That comes as no surprise to you. You can change your perceptions and probably have done so frequently in the past, and each time you change one of your perceptions, you congratulate yourself on being open to accepting reality, on your readiness to change.

What you probably have not considered is that if any one of your perceptions is not true, if you can change them, then maybe none of your perceptions are true. Let me repeat that: Maybe none of your perceptions are true. And if none of your perceptions are true then this means that your life is not real. This is a very important concept, so spend some time with me as I elaborate.

Your life is not real. It has never been real. It is a dream world. Your life, your reality, is a construct. You built it. You live in it, you experience it. Some parts of it you're happy about, many parts of it you are not. But it is all something that you have constructed and the wonderful liberating implication of this is that if you have constructed it, you can deconstruct it and make it up again, make it up into something that is much more to your liking. These are deep waters.

Here is a story which will make clear what I mean when I say that your life is not real, it's a construct. Read carefully and see if you can identify with either of the protagonists: Prakash watched through the window as Ram and his friends climbed into the fancy SUV. They were going to spend the winter break at Ram's home.

Or, rather, his family's farmhouse. Ram's father was a successful financier and lived well, very well. Prakash was not invited. 'He needs me to help him with his schoolwork but doesn't want to have anything to do with me outside class,' thought Prakash bitterly and the bile rose in his throat. Neither of Prakash's parents had gone to school. His mother was a domestic help. His father did odd jobs where he could find them – construction work, painting houses, cooking for parties. Both his parents fiercely valued education and were determined their son would do better than they had. By chance, his father discovered that the summer home whose lawn he had mowed belonged to the headmaster of an elite private school. Summoning all his courage, he begged him to do something for his son. The headmaster was a kindly man and summoned Prakash for an interview. The lad had raw intelligence and grim determination, and the headmaster felt an instinctive liking for him. He arranged for Prakash to come to his school on a scholarship. So, Prakash left home for the first time and went to an upper-class boarding school. Hard work never bothered him, and he grabbed the opportunity with both hands. Within a year, he was at the top of his class – an academic superstar. But social life was something else altogether. The scholarship paid for tuition, room and board, but very little was left over. He was also required to work in the school library, and this ate into his free time. He could not afford to hang out in pubs and bars and clubs with the others. They were all underage, but they drank anyway and had a good time and Prakash felt excluded.

Ram was his idol. Ram was handsome, opening batsman in the cricket team and a good tennis player. The other kids turned away when they saw Prakash's shabby clothing, winced when they heard his thick accent and ignored him. But Ram was always civil. Ram even asked Prakash's help in maths, and the two of them studied together and had long conversations. Once Ram invited Prakash out with a group of his friends. When they were at a restaurant, a talking head on the big screen television announced that a Princeton mathematician had solved Fermat's Enigma. Prakash was so enthralled that the others asked him what was up. He gave a brief discourse on the centuries-old mathematical puzzle that had not been resolved until now. He was so earnest that the others started tittering and the conversation then turned to girls and football. Ram never invited him out again. 'I should have known he was ashamed of me,' thought Prakash bitterly as he watched the SUV exit the school gates. A month later, Ram asked him if he would like to spend the weekend at his place. A thrill ran through Prakash. He was mistaken. Ram was not ashamed of him after all. 'Who else will be there?' Prakash asked excitedly. 'Why no one,' said Ram hesitantly, it'll just be the two of us. My parents are away, so we'll have the place to ourselves.' Prakash was enraged at the humiliation. He had been right all along. Ram did not want to be seen associating with him. This was his consolation prize for helping Ram with maths and physics and lab work. Ram was putting up with him for the weekend. 'No thanks,' he said and strode off. He was darned if he would accept such charity.

Prakash and Ram graduated and went their separate ways.

Years passed, but the hurt still rankled. Prakash became a partner at a prestigious consulting firm. He was invited to a meeting with the chief executive officer of a company that his firm was pitching to. He walked in well prepared and ran into Ram. Ram was the outside attorney called in by the chief executive officer specifically to evaluate the deal and bless it if it passed muster. A hot ball of lead formed inside Prakash and settled in his stomach. He knew he had no chance of landing the contract and seriously contemplated walking out. That would have been unprofessional, and he had his own team to consider. So, he went through the motions and summed up the many advantages to the client. When he finished, he skipped lunch and left the conference room immediately. He was washing up in the men's room when another figure slipped in. 'Ah, there you are,' said Ram. 'I was looking for you all over. Will you be personally supervising the project?'

'Yes,' said Prakash. 'I would have been,' he added quickly, to let Ram know that he knew it was dead. He was a big boy now and he could take his lumps and move on. But the molten ball of lead still remained. To his surprise, Ram grabbed his hand and pumped his arm up and down.

'How wonderful,' said Ram. 'This means we'll be working together again. I'll recommend that we give the contract to your firm immediately. Can you start next month?'

Ram forcibly took the bewildered Prakash to lunch, and they sat at a private table. 'It's so nice to run into you again like this,' said Ram and he seemed to be sincere. 'I admired you right through school. I could hit a hard red ball with a piece of wood, but you, you could really understand maths and physics and make them come alive.'

'Yeah,' said Prakash, both sceptical and bitter. 'How come you never wanted to be seen with me outside school?'

Ram did not pick up on the depth of emotion in Prakash's question.

'I was ashamed,' he confessed sheepishly. 'I thought if you knew how shallow my friends were and how frivolously we wasted time, you wouldn't want to work with me again. Remember the time you explained Fermats Enigma? I really wanted to know more, but those idiots couldn't understand the beauty of what you had just laid out. I wanted to be more like you, but I just didn't have what it takes. The theories and formulae never came alive to me except when you explained them. I went to a lot of trouble to engineer a weekend just for the two of us,' said Ram. 'I was hoping you'd explain some of those exercises you were working on that were way outside the syllabus, but you turned me down. I can understand that you didn't want to hang around with someone so far behind you,' continued Ram wistfully. 'But after all these years, it still hurts a little.'

This time it was Prakash who reached over to clasp Ram's hand. He felt light, unbearably light.

The burden he had been carrying for so many years simply dissolved.

'Let's make sure this project is a home run for the client,' said Prakash, and his eyes were moist.

Here are some questions for you to ponder.

Did Prakash need the second meeting with Ram to move into a different reality?

Was Ram being honest in what he said to Prakash? Does it matter?

Could Prakash have arbitrarily chosen to live in the second reality? Certainly, his life would have been a lot easier, his burden a lot lighter if he had chosen to do so.

These are deep waters that we are moving into. The notion that the reality we experience is a construct can be deeply unnerving. Perhaps it leaves you feeling as if the foundations of your life are being shaken, and you're right, they are being shaken. Do you feel that this is a risky course for you to venture on? Will it leave you in a vulnerable place? Perhaps, and especially if you are the type of person who needs validation from others. But the point of this book is to get you to a place where you don't need external validation, where the satisfaction and fulfilment you get out of life comes from within you. Perhaps you're wondering whether Prakash had constructed a reality with Ram, had really admired him and had wanted to be with him. What if it were not true? If you do this, will you live in a fake world, a world that will eventually shatter?

Let's think about this for a minute. There are two types of situations where this issue can arise. In the first situation, you don't have an ongoing relationship with the people involved and you'll never know whether it's true. So why not live as if the best possible scenario is true?

Let me give you another example to illustrate this. Assuming you're driving on a freeway and the traffic is heavy and suddenly a driver rushes past you, cuts into the lane in front of you, almost causing an accident and carries on in a reckless way, endangering other traffic as well. What is your instinctive reaction? Quite likely you'll be tempted to give him the finger. Quite possibly you will be intemperate in your speech and will stew and boil in frustrated anger. Now imagine that the person is driving in that reckless fashion because he has just learned that his son has been involved in an accident and is about to be operated on and he's desperately trying to get to the hospital in time. See how the second scenario causes all of the irritation to dissipate, and how you find yourself wishing that the person reaches the hospital in time.

Which is the better space for you to live in? Is the person a reckless driver or someone rushing to the hospital? You'll never know. How does it matter? Why not choose to live in this scenario, which leaves you in a better space.

That's one type of situation. In another type of situation, you may have an ongoing relationship with the person and perhaps there are actions you will take based upon your alternative reality, and those actions could have ramifications which could come back and hurt you if the alternative reality that you have chosen is not 'true'. If this is the situation, investigate whether the alternative reality has any basis, any foundation. Do it with a 'I don't know, but I will find out' attitude. But as you're doing it, give the person the benefit of the doubt and have as your default position the alternative reality that leaves you feeling better. Empowered. Uplifted. How you construct alternative realities will be explained to you in an exercise that I will take you through later.

Shifting your mental model can greatly affect your happiness. You are the sole person in charge of your happiness. But, too often, we imagine that others are, and we ascribe powers to these others. For example, when we think of our boss, we think about the control our boss has on our life. You think your boss can fire you. You think your boss can promote you. You think your boss can give you plum assignments, or you think your boss can give you horrible assignments that you don't want any part of. In short, he has tremendous power over you. But I suggest to you that when you have this as your mental model, you relate to your boss in a completely inauthentic and artificial way. The good that can come into your life does not come into your life because of your boss. Think of whatever happens to you as something sent to you by the universe. Your boss is the Blue Dart guy. The Blue Dart guy gives you your package, but you never imagine that the package comes from the Blue Dart guy. Do you thank the Blue Dart guy? Sure. You do. But you do not imagine that the package comes from the Blue Dart guy. The package comes from some place else. In exactly the same way, think of your boss as a Blue Dart guy. If you're to get a promotion, the promotion comes from the universe, not from your boss. Your boss is the instrument through which the promotion comes to you, but it doesn't come from your boss. Equally, if you are terminated, the notice of termination comes from the universe. Your boss is the instrument of termination, but again, it doesn't come from the boss. And as you do this, you will find that there is a feeling of liberation within you, and you relate to your boss in a completely different fashion than you do when you ascribe to your boss the capacity to make your life happy or miserable. This is a paradigm shift. As you consider it carefully, you will realise the immense power inherent in it.

Let me guide you through another journaling assignment to create an alternative reality. Find yourself a comfortable place to sit where you won't be disturbed. Go back to the journaling exercise we did earlier and pick one area that is troubling you. Don't pick the most difficult one right away. The reason for this is simple. It takes time and experience for you to gain success with this exercise, and if you pick the 800-pound gorilla in your life you may not be able to make much headway. But once you pick smaller problems and resolve them, you will be able to come back and defeat the 800-pound gorilla.

So, pick something which is important, but not necessarily the most difficult problem you're facing. Give a label to this reality and write it down on a new page. For example, you may be having a difficult time with your boss. Call it 'toxic boss'. Close your eyes for a minute and reflect on this area of your life. Imagine all of the details around that situation. Why do you think you have a toxic boss? What does he do that has a negative impact on your life? What have you done to resolve this situation and in what ways has this not worked? Now open your eyes and come up with a few possible alternative realities for the situation. Play around with different scenarios. Be creative. Is it possible that your boss has more projects than he can handle and is feeling overwhelmed? Label this 'overwhelmed boss' and write it down. Is it possible that your boss is having personal problems that you're not aware of, perhaps going through a divorce, perhaps dealing with children who are surly and distant? Label this 'boss plagued with personal problems' and write it down. Allow yourself to think of quite a few alternative realities. Remember, you have to devise ones that you can plausibly accept at some level. You cannot fool yourself. Pick an alternative reality that is easiest for you to accept. Take a minute or so and write down details about this alternative reality under the label that you have created. For example, if you put down 'overwhelmed boss', describe how your boss is unable to handle the responsibilities that have been assigned to him and the feeling of inadequacy, of being unable to cope, that he is experiencing.

Your homework for the next week is to live as if this alternative reality is true. If you're dealing with an overwhelmed boss, what will you do to express your sympathy and help him cope with the situation? If you're dealing with a boss plagued with personal problems, notice the waves of compassion that come out from you. Carefully note changes that arise in the situation itself, changes that arise in your emotional tenor as you interact with your boss and write them down in your journal below this alternative reality. Be gentle with yourself. Don't judge yourself, and especially don't judge yourself harshly. These are experiments. The more you do them, the more comfortable you will become in challenging your mental models. As you progress in this programme, you can come back to this exercise again and again, capturing new mental models and reconstructing the realities. They work for your professional situations; they work in your personal situations and any other concern that you may have.

Let me give you an example of a student of mine, Swati, who changed her relationship with her mother. Her mother lived abroad and visited her periodically and every time her mother visited, she would keep calling through the day to find out where she was and what she was doing and when she would be coming home. My student resented this intensely. She saw it as an unwarranted intrusion on her freedom and her privacy. She would snap back, and they would quarrel and she would feel guilty about being angry and getting into a fight. This generated a negative spiral, and she kept beating herself up for being so uncaring. At the same time, she harboured resentment at her freedom being restricted. It got to the point when she wished her mother would go back and she started feeling guilty about having such a wish. When she did the alternative reality exercise, she came up with a different scenario, one in which her mother was not being intrusive and did not wish to infringe on her freedom. Her mother was simply lonely and reaching out. She was saying pay attention to me, I exist, I am lonely. Swati actually started perceiving her mother as not a mother, but a child who needed attention. So, she took to calling her mother in advance to say, 'Hey, mom, I'm going out with some friends. I'm probably going to be back late. Why don't you have dinner and go for your walk? And don't worry about me. I'll see you when I get home.' It worked. The conversations stopped being acrimonious. They talked about important things that mattered to both of them. They were initially civil and then affectionate, and when the time came for her mother to go back, Swati actually regretted seeing her leave.

Let me give you another example of how the alternative reality exercise changed the life of one of my students. She was a highly compensated investment banker and worked for a demanding boss who was always grim-faced. The boss was also very critical and made a big deal of small errors of omission and commission. She decided that this was a great opportunity to play a game. Could she get her boss to smile and change some of his ways? If she could, she won. If she couldn't, he won.

She practised making jokes and made them work related. She jocularly let him know how she felt and suggested what he could do differently. She said things like, 'Hey Boss, I feel really bad when you pick on a spelling mistake I made and ignore the hours of work I put in so the financials look great. Can you, at least occasionally, tell me I did a great job?' It took a lot of courage for her to do this, but she persisted. In time her relationship with her boss improved and she mentally notched a 'win'. Her boss never knew of the 'game' she was playing but it made her uncomfortable situation more pleasant and sometimes even fun.

You can use the alternative reality exercise in virtually any situation that is troubling you right now. Personal situations, professional situations and relationships. Let me give you some tips on how you can go about doing this. It would be very helpful if you can put together a group of well-disposed friends who will help you come up with your alternative reality, because quite possibly they can see things that you might be eventually willing to accept but are unable to see on your own. If you do not have such a group of friends, you can very easily work on your own.

Describe as clearly as you can the situation that is troubling you, what you feel about it, why it exists. As you do so, you will recognise that you have made a number of assumptions. For example, the woman whose boss was a grouch assumed that he did not like her and that this trait was too entrenched to be influenced by anything she did. Both of these were assumptions, and neither of them were true. What assumptions are you making? Examine them carefully. Replace them with different assumptions and these different assumptions will automatically lead you to a different reality. Pick which one of these realities seems most natural for you. A reality which is better than the one you're experiencing and one that you can plausibly accept. And then start living life as if the alternative reality were true. As you start doing this, you will be amazed to discover the number of occasions when your alternative reality does in fact become your new reality. And that is the time for you to celebrate and then move on to apply this technique in another area of your life.

I have one final point for you to bear in mind. Let's go back to the two types of situations we talked about before. In the first type of situation you are interacting with persons whom you may never meet again and there is relatively little, if any, downside in coming up with an alternative reality and living in it. Come up with the best one that you can and live in it with joy and gusto. In the second situation, you have an ongoing relationship with the persons involved, and if you come up with an alternative reality and it does not fit the circumstances, you might take actions which might actually come back and harm you. In such situations, what you do is create the alternative reality. Give the other person the benefit of the doubt. Start living in that alternative reality. But check it out very carefully. Start off with the best possible scenario and check it carefully to find out if it has a basis in fact. If it does, well and good and you're home free. If it doesn't, explore the boundaries until you can come up with another alternative reality, which does in fact hold water and is in fact better than the one you are presently experiencing.

To drive the point home further, let me share another story with you. It's an example of how misreading a situation can cause intense emotional agony. One of my students, Suresh, was promoted as the head of operations of his company in the United Kingdom. He was a senior executive. There were nine executives of similar rank who basically ran the company's operations all over Europe. There was a special committee consisting of four of them, who set strategy for all of Europe and sometimes their actions also had an impact on the company headquarters in the United States. Shortly after Suresh took on his new role, a vacancy appeared on that committee and he expected to be nominated. His boss did not nominate him. Suresh immediately felt that his boss did not like him and the more he thought about it, the more convinced he was that that was true. He noticed that his emails were not getting replied to. He found it difficult to get a meeting with his boss. He did not feel that he got the guidance that he expected. He started having sleepless nights. He was concerned about whether he would be retained in his job. He was debating whether he should search for another job. He was not quite an emotional wreck, but he was very, very concerned and stressed.

During the alternative reality exercise, his team suggested that he was greatly misreading the situation. The alternative reality he came up with was, 'My boss really has my best interests at heart and wants me to succeed. He did not nominate me to the committee because I had just been promoted to my present role and he wanted me to be completely familiar with it and learn the ropes before I take on additional responsibility. So, by not appointing me to the committee, he was actually looking after my interests. As for not responding to my emails or meeting with me, everybody has more stuff on their plate than they can handle and he's simply too busy and the fact that he didn't respond to my emails means nothing except that he didn't respond to my emails. Suresh started living as if this were the reality. He felt better immediately and approximately ten days after that, he was at an off-site meeting with his boss and they went out for drinks after the day's work was done. During the course of the evening he casually asked, 'By the way, why didn't you nominate me to that committee?' And his boss said, 'I wanted you to get familiar with your new role before

I did that. I'm looking forward to working with you, and I didn't want you to be out of your depth by handling more responsibility than you were ready for. Do you feel that you're capable of handling the additional responsibility?' And Suresh said, 'Yes.' So, his boss said, 'Fine, there'll be another vacancy coming up in the next two months, and I'll nominate you at that time.'

And he did. So, all of the emotional agony that Suresh put himself through was unnecessary. Can you see how Suresh's mental models produced emotional reactions that could have caused him to take a harmful action in response? What if he had actually sought out another position, and perhaps even accepted it? On the other hand, what if this person was correct about his perception? Would his actions have been justified? Imagine if you were this person, would you have been living your ideal reality if you had taken the actions this person was contemplating? Would you have been living in control of your own happiness? Whenever you are confronted with a similar situation, don't take any action that could potentially come back and harm you, in case you were mistaken in your estimation. Construct an alternative reality for yourself. Start living as if this alternative reality were the reality and, at the earliest opportunity, run a check on whether or not your reality is working. You will be surprised at how many times your alternative reality will work. And the few times that it doesn't, just chalk it up to that's the way the world is and move on from there. You've done a great job so far and we've begun challenging some very heavy perceptions.

3

Living in Awareness

You've learned about mental chatter and mental models and have an idea of how they shape your reality. Take a deeper look at the current reality of your own life. This is the 'reality' that you are experiencing. Are you satisfied with your current reality? How do you feel about your relationships? How do you feel about your career? How do you feel about your time management?

Quite likely you desire a change in some or all of these areas and the good news, the really good news is that you can change your reality. In order to alter your reality, we have to revisit your mental chatter. You need to understand that it won't go away. It's there. You're stuck with it. The harder you try to stop it, the louder it becomes. Think of a wild horse that's standing by itself in the middle of a field. If you creep up on it, it runs away. If you succeed in coming up to it and try to saddle it, it starts galloping. That's your mind. You can't still it.

But that's not entirely bad news. Mental chatter is not your enemy. Think of your mind as a fertile piece of ground. When you plant a seedling and give it proper nutrients and water it regularly, it will grow into a healthy tree. It's very important for you to realise that what you put into your mind is what will grow and magnify. Here is something for you to think about. Imagine a plot of fertile land. You weed it, you till it, you add topsoil to it and you're ready to make a vegetable garden. And then something happens, and you have to go away. If you come back in a couple of months, you will be amazed at how many weeds there are and how choked it is. If you come back after ten years, you'll be amazed at what a forest has grown in your absence. That's your mind. You have not been conscious of your mental chatter. Your awareness has been absent. You have been an absentee landlord for decades. Why should you be so surprised that such a forest, such a wild, uncontrolled jungle has grown between your ears?

Let me begin by showing you how to resolve this. The first step is to filter and cultivate the seeds that germinate in your mind. Let me introduce you to the witness. The witness is the dispassionate observer, a mirror of your mental chatter. In fact, the witness is often referred to as the witness consciousness in eastern contemplative practices such as in Zen Buddhist philosophy. Can you right now observe your own mind and determine whether you're feeling happy or sad and whether your mind is agitated? It is the witness who is observing this. Think of the witness as an entity suspended a foot above your head who simply notes down everything that you think and do dispassionately.

It does not pass judgement. It simply observes and records.

To gain a more practical understanding of the witness, I would like to guide you through a brief practice called the awareness practice. Find a comfortable place where you won't be disturbed. Sit with your back straight and feet flat or crossed on the floor. Close your eyes. Begin to take a few deep breaths. Feel yourself relaxing. Let your awareness go to the soles of your feet. Clench your toes and then unclench them and let them relax. Take your attention to your ankles. Flex them. Relax them. Go to your calf muscles and then your thighs. Consciously relax your muscles. Move upwards. How are your hips? Feel the weight of your body on your hips, on your chair. See how your hips are sinking into the cushion. Focus on them and let them relax. Move to your stomach. Contract your stomach muscles. Expand your stomach. Let it go. Feel your stomach relax. Move up to your chest. Contract your pectoral muscles. Relax them. Contract them again. Relax them again. Let them stay relaxed. Imagine them sinking down. Move your focus to your arms, your hands. Where are your fingers? Lay them gently on your thighs. Let them relax. Tense your forearm muscles. And then your biceps and triceps. And relax them and let them stay relaxed.

Think of your body like a rag doll. See how a rag doll lies on the floor. Completely at ease. Completely flexible, completely relaxed. Imagine that you are like that rag doll. Let all of your limbs, every part of yourself, have the same ease. Go to your face. Close your eyes and clench them tight. Then relax. But keep them closed. Clench your jaw. Tighten your cheek muscles. And let them go. Wrinkle your forehead. Let that go. Go back to thinking about the rag doll. See how the rag doll lies on the floor. Completely unmoving. Completely natural. Completely relaxed. Imagine yourself like that doll. You are completely relaxed. You're breathing slowly. And now, gradually bring your attention from your body to your breath. Become aware of the breath coming into your nostrils, travelling through your nasal passages and into your lungs. Slowly, easily, start breathing abdominally using your entire thoracic cavity. Let your stomach expand outwards as you take a breath in and let it contract in to force the breath out. As you do this, your breathing will become even slower. Let it. Just focus on your breath. Breathe in. Breathe out. Breathe in. Breathe out.

As you do this, you will find thoughts arise in your mind. Very soon you will be distracted from watching your breath. What do you have to do? Will you be able to accomplish all that is necessary? As these distracting thoughts come to your mind, let them go. Imagine that your thoughts are like clouds. And the clouds are passing through a rake. And the rake doesn't catch the clouds. The clouds just pass through the rake. You're like that. There are thoughts and they come and they go and you observe them and you're not drawn to any of them. Breathe in. Breathe out. Very often you will find that a thought comes, and you become enraptured with it, and you've forgotten to mind your breathing. Your mental chatter has just carried you away. The moment you become aware that you have lost your focus, come back to your breathing. Don't beat yourself up about it. No guilt feelings. Just become aware that you have been carried away by your mental chatter, detach yourself gently and come back. Breathe in. Breathe out. Breathe in. Breathe out. Be conscious of your stomach. It moves out as you breathe in. It moves in as you breathe out. Breathe in. Breathe out. Breathe in. Breathe out. Consciously, curiously, with love and compassion watch the thoughts that pass through your mind. Notice how many there are and how quickly they succeed each other. But don't get carried away by them. Simply observe them. Breathe in. Breathe out. Breathe in. Breathe out. Each thought is a cloud, and the cloud will pass through the open teeth of the rake, and it will not get caught in the rake. Observe the thoughts but don't let any of them carry you away. And as you do that you will find that all of the things which concerned you, all of the things which evoked strong emotions in you, have suddenly become powerless to affect your emotional well-being.

You are the witness, the dispassionate observer. Breathe in. Breathe out. Breathe in. Breathe out. Breathe in. Breathe out. Breathe in. Breathe out. Gently direct your attention back to your body. Are you conscious of your hips on your chair? Are you conscious of your feet on the floor? Are you conscious of your palms on your thighs? Imagine your attention like a torch and you can focus the torch anywhere you want. Focus it gently on the various parts of your body and then focus it back on your breathing. Breathe in. Breathe out.

Gently return your attention to the room that you're in. Keep breathing slowly and gently open your eyes. That which noticed the breathing, that which became aware that it was no longer noticing the breathing – that is the witness. How difficult was it for you to maintain your focus on your breath? Did you find that you had been lost in thought long before you even recognised it? If so, there is no cause for discouragement. When you first start practising finding your witness, you will lose your witness very fast; perhaps within seconds. This is normal. Every time you realise you have lost your witness, find it again and bring it back. You will probably find it most convenient to think of the witness as the same gender as you are. If you're a woman and you lose the witness, find her. If you're a man and you lose the witness, find him and observe your breathing. Breathe in. Breathe out. Breathe in. Breathe out.

What you will notice is that as you practise finding the witness it becomes easier and easier for you to recover her when she gets lost. You can cultivate your relationship with the witness in everyday life. You don't need to sit in meditation to do it. Observe your emotional tenor. Are you happy? Are you sad? Train yourself. So that whenever you are troubled by strong emotions – hatred, anger, jealousy, depression – you move immediately into the witness mode. You will find that as you identify with the witness, emotions will become weaker. They are much less likely to sweep you away. You are much more able to deal with them. Gradually you will reach a plateau where you are serene. And you will find that you're experiencing peace.

Keep practising this. To help you cultivate your witness awareness, here is a practice-focused intent that you can try on your own. Get out your journal once more and take notes on this. Label the page 'focused intent'. Pick one day this week, perhaps tomorrow, and commit to doing all of your activities with the same focused intent as you used to watch your breath. Start as soon as you wake up. Become aware of your thoughts immediately. Do you wish that you could sleep some more? Are you glad that the day has begun? Just become aware of your emotional tenor. When you brush your teeth be aware that you're brushing your teeth. Notice the flavour of the toothpaste on your brush. Feel the massage that the brush is giving your gums. Feel your teeth getting clean.

As you dress for the day, focus on each garment as you put it on. Be aware that you're buttoning your shirt, combing your hair, putting on your shoes. As you're eating breakfast be conscious of each spoonful that you convey to your mouth.

Recognise that by some magic you don't understand what you're eating is being converted into muscle and sinew and blood and nourishing you. This is a divine activity. Recognise it. Honour it.

When you are driving, be aware of the road, the vehicles on the road, cars on either side of you. Accomplish your tasks one at a time. No multitasking. No checking your email while you talk on the phone and read a report at the same time. Stay completely in the moment when you're speaking with another person. Look them in the eye. Observe their facial expressions. What is being conveyed by the way they interact, the intonation of their voice?

Imagine your life is an hourglass. There are grains of sand below, all of the time that has already passed. There are grains of sand above, all of the years and hours and days left to you. No matter how hard you shake the hourglass, only one grain of sand at a time goes through the neck. That grain is the instant at hand. Focus on it. Let your witness observe your mental chatter throughout the day. Do things unhurriedly. I said unhurriedly, not slowly. Hurry is in your mind. Write down your experience in your journal. You will find that it is extraordinarily difficult to be mindful for even a day. In all likelihood, you will lose your witness fifty or more times an hour.

Do not be discouraged. This is normal. The bad news is that you will never succeed in being completely mindful. The good news, the wonderful news, is that even a slight increase in mindfulness will bring a quantum improvement in your life. You will find that you have become exponentially more effective if you can imagine yourself as a container of golden energy. Your attention is in that golden liquid. And you pour this golden energy over the task that you have at hand. Visualise this dramatically, and you will find the task goes smoother, that you are more efficient and more effective. Discover this for yourself.

Once you begin consciously filtering what you let into your mind, you can use a universal law that I call the law of increase. The law of increase is one of those immutable laws, somewhat like the law of gravity. The law of increase states that that which we truly appreciate and are grateful for will increase in our life. When we can focus on something and appreciate it with all our heart and the gratitude for having it in our life wells out and overflows, we will find that more and more of it will automatically appear in our life. Perhaps this may be a big conceptual leap for some of you who do not believe that the universe possesses an intelligence. But it does. You will discover it for yourself as you apply this law. Think of how you are already proving this true in your own life. Do you feed your fears and insecurities about work and family? If you do, you will find that they are multiplied, and they come back to you.

One of the most powerful exercises that you can do is the appreciation and gratitude exercise. Let me guide you through this. But before I do, let me tell you what I have observed. In every class that I teach, there are between six and ten students who suffer from insomnia. They go to bed at night, but they cannot fall asleep. They toss, they turn. They're emotionally drained. In 100 per cent of the cases, they have reported back to me that after trying the appreciation and gratitude exercise they went to bed, slept soundly and woke up refreshed, more refreshed than they could remember for a long time. That's what appreciation and gratitude can do for you. But that's only a small part of what they can do for you.

Let's get started.

Once again, find a comfortable place where you won't be disturbed. Sit with your back straight and feet flat or crossed on the floor. Close your eyes. Take a few deep breaths. Let yourself relax. Think back to yesterday. Starting with the time you woke up in the morning, before you even got out of bed Was there something for you to be thankful about? Perhaps it was that you woke up to live another day. Perhaps it was that you woke up in a comfortable warm bed. Perhaps because you woke up next to a person you love. Find at least one aspect that you could truly be thankful for. Carry on and recall the process of getting ready for your day. Find something else to be thankful for. Perhaps it was that you don't have to be concerned about having food to eat, that you can take a warm shower, that you have adequate clothing, that there was a song you liked playing on the radio.

Now, recall the tasks of your day. Find another aspect to be thankful for. Perhaps it was that you got a call from an old friend. A co-worker complimented you. You finished a project that you had been working on for a long time. Fast forward to the end of your day. You're back home. What is there for you to be grateful for? A nice dinner with the family. The ability to relax at the end of a long day. A favourite television programme to watch. Now, remember the moment when your head hit the pillow just before you closed your eyes.

Review in your mind all of the wonderful things that occurred in your day that you have to be grateful for: the warm shower or project completed, a safe drive home, a nice dinner with your loved one. Genuinely connect with this feeling of deep appreciation and gratitude. Let it start from the soles of your feet and move up through your body until it overflows through your mouth and your ears and your eyes. Broadcast it out as a statement of who you are. Connect with this feeling of gratitude and gradually let the storyline of why you are grateful go. Simply feel gratitude, not in particular for anything. Let it envelop you and become a statement of who you are before you gently close your eyes and drift off to a peaceful sleep. Now, gently return your attention back to the room that you're in. Take a few deep breaths. Open your eyes.

This practice is merely a starting point for cultivating a heart of gratitude. You begin by feeling gratitude for something in your life. But as you continue your practice, I would like you to connect with the feeling of gratitude itself, not gratitude for any particular circumstances, but simply with the feeling of gratitude. Let this become a part of your existence, a statement of who you are and have become.

Now that you know how to summon the feeling of gratitude, I would like you to try an assignment. Homework, if you will. You might find it helpful to take your journal out and take notes on this homework: Appreciation and gratitude for the day. At the end of the evening, just before you go to sleep, connect with the general feeling of gratitude. If you have a difficult time connecting, recall the elements of your day that you can be grateful for and use that as a launching pad for connecting with the feeling of gratitude. Once you feel the connection, drop the storylines, the circumstances of why you are being grateful. Simply be grateful. You can do this exercise lying down, but many report that it is so relaxing they fall asleep before completing it. If you find this happens in your case, try sitting up in bed until you finish the exercise and then lie down. Pay attention to your mental chatter the following morning as soon as you awake. You will notice that your mental chatter is a lot quieter and more peaceful than it normally is. Reinforce this by summoning the feeling of gratitude again. Notice any changes in your emotional tenor during the day.

Once you have practised this for a week, take it a step further and regularly connect with the feeling of gratitude throughout the day. Push gently, but don't force it. Use your entire body. When you smile, feel the muscles on your face smiling. Walk with a spring in your step. Hum a happy tune. Let the feeling radiate out from you and envelop others with whom you are interacting. Genuinely wish them well. Wish them all the best in life. Wish that they too can experience gratitude and peace. Perhaps you may be wondering how practising appreciation and gratitude causes the law of increase to work in your life. It begins by refocusing your attention on the positive aspects of your life, instead of the negative, the things that you complain about. It makes it easier for you to recognise the miracles that are constantly occurring in your life on a daily basis.

As you practise appreciation and gratitude, you can increase the number of miracles that happen in your life. It's important for you to understand what I mean by a miracle. It is not necessary for a miracle to violate the laws of physics. It is not necessary for a miracle to be a grand and rare event like Krishna lifting the Govardhan mountain or Hanuman flying to Lanka. For a miracle to happen in your life, only one thing is necessary – that you have a deep feeling that the universe has intervened for you and on your behalf. And if you practise appreciation and gratitude, you will find a steady stream of miracles occurring in your life. Don't make the mistake of labelling a miracle a coincidence. The primary difference between a miracle and a coincidence is how you view it – your perspective.

Let me share a personal example with you. I had been aware of a particular publisher for quite some time and had the feeling that a programme with that publisher was an ideal way to get my work out to people who needed it. When I left to teach at London Business School, I left a catalogue from that publisher on my table as a reminder for me to contact the company on my return. I did not mention this to my agent. While I was in London, my agent negotiated a contract for me with that same publisher and by the time I came back to New York, all that was left for me to do was sign the contract. Is this a coincidence or a miracle? If I label it a coincidence, I live in a world where random things happen unpredictably. Not a bad place to be. But if I label it a miracle, it is another example of a benevolent universe working in my interest and manifesting what is best for me and for others. That is so much nicer a house to dwell in. So, you have a choice. You can live in a world where coincidences happen and some of them are not nice perhaps, or you can live in a world where miracles happen and they're always nice. I suggest that it's far better for you to live in a world where miracles happen, and as you start living in such a world, you will discover that you can actually create miracles. You'll probably begin by creating small miracles, and as you gain experience, you can create bigger and bigger miracles.

Look at your life, at the events that have happened in the past and things that are happening right now. Look for fortuitous coincidences, things that you would normally have dismissed, and consider if they were in fact miracles. Use the law of increase to create miracles. Remember that your reality is only one possible reality. You can change it. The universe is a conscious entity and it will respond to your input. Think of it as a dance. You and the universe are intricately intertwined. And if you lead in a different direction, it has no choice but to respond in kind. So, pay close attention.

Expect miracles to happen. When shopping, expect to find that the item you're looking for will be on sale. When working, expect that when you are stuck on a difficult project, someone will come by who will have precisely the information you need and be willing to share it with you. When playing chess, expect that when you are in a difficult position, you will be able to spot a winning combination. Do this throughout the day whenever you remember. Don't be disappointed when it doesn't happen. Pay attention to the number of times it does happen. And as you do, you will find that the number of occasions when it does happen increases. Yes, miracles are increasing in your life and you should note each one of these as well as your emotional undertone in your journal.

We've taken some big conceptual leaps in this chapter and I congratulate you for your willingness to step into the unknown. I highly encourage you to do the exercises as I have assigned before you move on to the next chapter.

4

Eliminate the Stress in Your Life

In this chapter, I'm going to give you some suggestions which will help you eliminate most of the stress in your life. All of the stress in your life is caused by the fact that the universe presents you with circumstances you don't like, and you are not ready to accept it. Let me repeat that. Not some of the stress, not most of the stress; all of the stress in your life is caused by your inability to accept what the universe is presenting you with.

Imagine this situation: you have an important business meeting. You're in a cab, hurrying, you're running late and there's a traffic jam, and you seem to meet red lights at every intersection. What are your emotions? Seething rage, frustration, anger. There are two parts to it. On the one hand, you're beating yourself up for doing it again and for not arranging your affairs so that you could leave earlier and, on the other hand, you're railing against the red lights, the traffic, the slow driver – unmitigated stress.

All of these have to do with your expectations, which are not being met. You have expectations about how other people should behave. You have expectations about what the outcome should be for any action that you take. You have expectations about how others will treat you and about how any outcome will affect you. Since expectations which are not met lead to stress in your life, you might be tempted to experiment with removing expectations. Try it. It will not take you long to find out that this is impossible. Every action that you take has an expectation embedded in it somewhere. Every action!

If you scratch your nose, it is with the expectation that the itch will go away. It is impossible for you to give up expectations. But it is possible for you to react differently when your expectations are not met. And they will not be met many times, perhaps even most of the time. When you can accept an outcome regardless of whether or not it is something you wanted, you will find that the stress eases away from your life.

Let's look at this a little bit deeper. Understand that you have some control over your actions. Not complete control, but a great deal. You have no control at all over the outcome. You take actions and you expect outcome A. Sometimes you get it and you're happy. More often you'll get outcome B, C, D or E. You might even get outcome F which is the exact opposite of what you would have liked. What happens when that occurs? Typically, you rail against it. You're angry, you're frustrated, you're depressed. You simply add stress to your life. If you can embrace the outcome, whatever it is, you will find that you are more effective in dealing with the situation. You will also find that regardless of the circumstances, you remain in a calm, serene place.

Acceptance is not passive. Let's say that you have been working long hours. You have come home at bedtime, skipping dinner. You've been missing family get-togethers and occasions. So, one evening you decide to bring flowers home to your wife as a gesture of goodwill. Perhaps she will receive them gratefully and you'll have a deep conversation, and your relationship will improve or perhaps she will rage at you. 'So now you finally remember me. Who are you having an affair with?' And the next thing you know, you have a full-blown marital scrap. Or perhaps you find that your son is distant, immersed in his own life and you ask him: How are you doing? What happened at school today? This could lead to a deep conversation, or he could snap at you for intruding into his life. Actions are within your control. The outcome is not.

Let me begin by showing you how to resolve this. The first step is to control how you react emotionally and what you do when your expectation is not met. You have already begun learning the skills that will help you with this. The witness is your friend. You can begin to use the witness to notice your reactions to unmet expectations. Remember when you are in the witness state, you note your reactions with detachment. You do not pass judgement. You're like a tennis umpire.

I'd like to guide you through a practice that will help you begin to learn to start witnessing difficult experiences.

Once again, find a comfortable place where you will not be disturbed. Sit with your back straight, feet flat or crossed on the floor. Close your eyes and take a few deep breaths. Feel yourself relax. Imagine that you are a trauma surgeon in a busy hospital. You witness horrifying traumas, accident victims, knife wounds, drug overdoses, burn injuries. You have to act quickly because there is a constant stream of patients coming. When a critically wounded patient arrives on your operating table, you do what you have to. This is the witness. The trauma surgeon does not get emotionally involved with the situation of her patient. She does what she needs to do. Sometimes the operation is successful, sometimes it is not, but she does what she has to do and then she moves on. If a surgeon becomes emotionally involved with the patient, she will be far less effective and in fact she might even become dangerous. This is the reason why surgeons are not permitted to operate on their family members.

Come back to your present life and think of a difficult situation that you are facing. Perhaps it's around work or a relationship, money or family. Now, reconnect with your witness. Be like a trauma surgeon. The situation has not changed. It is still a difficult situation, but now you're observing it, detached unemotionally. What needs to be done? Think of some possible ways to deal with this situation. What are the probable outcomes and which approach do you think will lead to the best overall outcome for all involved?

Take a few deep breaths. Come back to the room you're in. Open your eyes. This is a practice that you can use again and again to begin cultivating your inner witness. As I said before, you will probably find it most helpful to think of your witness as the same gender as you are. The witness can heal you, but you cannot force them to come or to stay. So, be gentle with yourself when you are working on difficult circumstances. If you have a wound, a scab will form on it. You can pick at the scab, but it won't fall off until the wound is healed. If you pick it before the wound is healed, you will have another wound, and soon another scab will form. It's the same way with the witness. If he disappears, call him back gently. The bad news is that it is very easy to lose the witness when you identify with your emotions and the situation that you are in. Don't be discouraged. Because the good news is that even a modest amount of success in identifying with the witness will bring a profound improvement in your life. With practice, you will find that every time you are in a turbulent situation, when you are being swept away by negative emotions, you can immediately access the witness and even a few minutes in that space will bring healing. This is a learnable skill. It's no different from learning to ride a bicycle. You just have to practice.

Some of you may be asking how do I work with the terrible circumstances not in my own life, which I feel I can control, but the circumstances of the world, for example genocide, slavery, war, disease. The answer to this is, whenever you find yourself emotionally affected, especially if you find yourself strongly affected, you have to do something. Bob Dylan, in his hit song 'Blowin' in the Wind', asks, 'How many times can a man turn his head and pretend that he just doesn't see?' When you contemplate the scale of disaster and suffering in the world, it is very easy to be overwhelmed.

Where should you devote your attention and effort, to genocide in places like Darfur, to war victims in Afghanistan and Iraq and other places, to persons suffering from AIDS in South Africa, in India, in many countries around the world, child slavery, labour exploitation.

There is so much wrong in the world today and you feel so helpless, so powerless. There is a tendency to react to this by throwing up your hands in despair and withdrawing. This does not serve you well. Here is a better way for you to cope. Pick any/only one situation that really troubles you. Read up about it, become knowledgeable, understand what the scope of the problem is, understand who are the people who are working to ameliorate it, and then reach out to do your bit. Set limits on yourself. How much time you can devote, how much money you can contribute, and within the parameters that you have laid out for yourself be as effective as you can. For example, if you are disturbed by an animal abuse story in the news, ask yourself what you can do to help lessen animal abuse. Donate your time. Call the local shelter and adopt an abused animal. Donate money. Perhaps you're most affected by child slavery and labour practices. You might pick a particular industry, say, the carpet industry, in which these practices are rife. You could lobby department stores not to buy carpets produced by child labour. You could affiliate with organisations which are devoted to liberating child slaves and providing them with housing and educational opportunities. You could lobby for legislation to prevent companies from importing products produced by child labour. You could do some of these or all of these. You pick, but if you are disturbed, pick a cause and do something concrete.

If you have been doing the exercises suggested, you will by now have realised that gratitude has a tremendous impact on how you feel. It affects you. It affects those around you. How can you practise gratitude for an unexpected outcome? There is always something to be grateful for. Here is a chance to use your creativity. For example, you look forward to a romantic date and she brings her brother along. This is not what you expected, but be thankful for the fact that you have an opportunity to make a new friend. Perhaps one who could even help you further your suit. It is the notion of gratitude welling up that will prevent this situation from becoming one that stresses you out and makes you an emotional basket case. Let gratitude be with you at all times. Look carefully at how you react to circumstances in your life. What was the first thing that you did when your date showed up with her brother in tow? What you did is you immediately stuck a label on it, 'this is bad' – that's what we do all the time. We are confronted with an outcome, and we label it, this is good, this is bad. We tend to use the bad label much more often than we tend to use the good label. Recognise that the moment you stick a label on an outcome, that is exactly how you experience it.

An ancient Sufi story is very instructive. There was a man and his son, and they lived in a valley. They were poor, very poor, and the man decided that he would try to make a living in a different profession. He would breed horses. So, he sold all his worldly goods and borrowed money and bought a stallion. He put the stallion in the paddock and went to bed, and the next morning the stallion had knocked the top bar down and disappeared. All of his friends, his neighbours, clustered around him, clucking in sympathy. 'Oh, how terrible you went into debt. You bought a stallion and now the stallion is gone. You have lost all means of livelihood.' 'How bad! How bad! How terrible!' And the old man looked at them and said, 'Good thing, bad thing, who knows?'

In a week's time, the stallion fell in with a group of wild horses and the wild horses came to the valley where the man lived, and he was able to entice them into his paddock, which he had fixed. So, now he had his stallion back, plus a dozen wild horses that could be trained and sold. Once again, his friends and neighbours clustered around congratulating him on his good fortune and he looked them in the eye and said, 'Good thing, bad thing, who knows?'

The man and his son started training the horses. The son was on the stallion one day when it bucked and threw him. The stallion stomped on his leg, the leg broke, and it eventually healed crooked. He would never walk without a limp again, and the neighbours clustered around, clucking in sympathy. 'How terrible such a young man, so handsome, how will he now marry or find a wife?' The man looked them in the eye and said, 'Good thing, bad thing, who knows?'

That summer, the king of the country declared war and press gangs moved through the countryside inducting all the young men into the army. The old man's son was spared because of his game leg. The villagers who had lost members of their own family, clustered around him weeping, 'How terrible our situation but how fortunate are you,

you still have your son. We don't know if we will ever see our sons back.' And the old man looked them in the eye and said, 'Good thing, bad thing, who knows?', and so it goes on and on.

Look back on your life. Look back on events and outcomes that in the past you labelled 'bad'. With the wisdom of hindsight, can you see that some of the things that you labelled bad were really not so terrible. Can you see that some of them might actually have been pretty good things. For example, there was a time in my life when I held a managerial position. It was quite stressful and very time-consuming. I frequently felt overwhelmed. I took decisions that affected other people, and because I had no time, or thought I had no time, I did not consult them. They resented this. They tried to explain this to me, but I was too busy to listen. Shortly thereafter, I faced a workplace coup. They conspired and revolted. They spoke to my boss, and I was dumped. I felt terrible. My ego was hurt. I moped, but there was an unexpected consequence. All of a sudden, I had a lot of free time, and I used this free time to start a project that succeeded beyond my wildest imagination. It was the best thing that could have happened to me. With further hindsight, even the blow to my ego was something I badly needed. This wasn't a bad thing at all. It was an unadulterated good thing. But it took me a long time to realise this.

In your life, you will be confronted with outcomes that you do not expect and perhaps outcomes that you do not want. Your tendency will be to label this a bad thing. Stop. You don't know whether this is a bad thing or a good thing. You will not know for many years. Perhaps you will never know. So, why not label it a good thing? Let this be your default position. When you label everything that happens to you as a good thing you will be amazed at how you chart your life so that it does in fact become a good thing. Practise this. Here is a reflection that might help.

Find a comfortable place where you won't be disturbed and sit with your back straight and feet crossed or flat on the floor. Close your eyes. Begin to take a few deep breaths. Feel yourself relaxing. Recall an event that has occurred in your life within the last five years that you originally labelled a bad thing. An event that eventually turned out to be a blessing. Perhaps it was a bad relationship, losing a job, an accident or a missed opportunity. Recall any stress you may have felt when you initially experienced the event. Now, fast forward to the circumstances that caused this so-called bad event to seem more like a blessing. What happened to change your perspective on what you had originally labelled a bad event? Open your eyes and come back to the present moment. Write it all down. What happened initially to make you think it was 'bad'. What changed to lead you to the conclusion that it was actually good.

This exercise is a straightforward way of showing us that we simply don't know whether whatever has happened to us is good or bad. Our lives are constantly changing and we cannot control the outcomes of those changes, but we can control our reactions to those outcomes. Let me repeat. Since you don't know whether what has happened to you is good or bad; when you won't know for years and will perhaps never know; why not simply label something as good? This will unleash forces that in fact lead you to experience it as good.

Some of you might be wondering if I'm advocating positive thinking. I am not. In positive thinking, you decide that something is bad and then you decide that you will consider positive aspects of it and make the best of a bad job. I'm asking you to go beyond that. I'm asking you to consider a different mental model. I am asking you to recognise that you are never given a lemon from which you make lemonade, but rather what you are given is the continuous opportunity to make lemonade. Not only are you being given the continuous opportunity to make lemonade, you're being given the opportunity to franchise lemonade stands throughout the world and build a huge empire based on lemonade. Is it true that you are never handed a lemon, but only the opportunity to make lemonade? What about really horrible events that could happen in life, loss of a job, death of a spouse, serious injury or illness? It is very difficult for us to conceive of any of these as good things. Perhaps. But don't be in a hurry to label them as bad things. Recognise that you do not know. Be open to the possibility that in some way they could be good things and this will be revealed to you in the fullness of time as your life progresses. When you are open to this possibility, you will not be overwhelmed or become dysfunctional with grief and gradually you will discover that your intent does bring about a more satisfactory outcome. You will only succeed in doing this if you adopt this framework, this mental model, long before disastrous events confront you.

Any action we take is linked with the expectation of a particular outcome. We become attached to the outcome. If the outcome is what we wanted, we feel elated. If the outcome is different from what we wanted, we feel angry, frustrated and depressed. As mentioned before, this is the cause of all of the stress in our life. There is an antidote to this, a powerful antidote. It is surrender. Surrender is a powerful way to develop personal mastery over our reactions to any outcome. When you surrender, you acknowledge that there is a power greater than you, a power that you cannot begin to comprehend with your limited intelligence and awareness. Some of you might feel comfortable thinking of a divine being. For our purposes, we will refer to this greater power as the universe and the universe is sentient, as we will discuss later. We do not surrender to a person. We surrender to the universe. But what is surrender? Surrender is the formal acknowledgement that our intelligence and abilities are limited. We do not know what is in our best interests or the best interests of those close to us or the world at large. We use what abilities and knowledge we have to decide that a particular outcome is desirable. It may be, it may not be, but we don't have perfect knowledge. The universe, on the other hand, does have perfect knowledge and if we acknowledge that, we are surrendering. Surrender and acceptance go hand in hand. They are inextricably linked. So, we do our dance, we take our actions, we expect an outcome, and we may get it or we may not. But if we accept, if we gratefully embrace whatever outcome we are actually confronted with, then we are surrendering.

Surrendering is not weakness. It is not passive. In fact, it is resolutely active. You are merely surrendering to the don't know aspect of 'good thing', 'bad thing', 'don't know'. The truth is you will never definitively know, so why not choose your reality and live without the stress. You're actually surrendering your own agenda for the outcome that you want. So, when the universe presents you an outcome which is different from what you expected and wanted, you have to accept it. This is why surrender and acceptance are linked. The outcome that you are facing was provided to you by a sentient universe and therefore, in some way that you cannot fathom, is perfect. So, you accept it gratefully, you embrace it. But having embraced it, you are still a human being, confronting a world around you and you want to make changes in that world. This is a new beginning for you. You take more actions to achieve your desired outcome. Perhaps the outcome you now desire is the same one that you did before and your reaction is the same with redoubled vigour, or perhaps you want to take a different set of actions or shoot for a different outcome. It doesn't matter. It is a new beginning. And whatever happens as a result of the actions you now take, you surrender and accept as before and you repeat this process. This is what you will do for the rest of your life. You may think this is a paradox. How can you desire an outcome, take actions with that desired outcome in mind and then surrender and then accept an outcome which is different from what you desired. It may seem difficult, but will become easier as you begin to practice surrender.

How do we begin surrendering and accepting any outcome? Here is a three-step process. The first is intention. Take all of your actions with a clear knowledge of your intention. What exactly is it that you would like to have happen? As you did with the earlier exercise of creating miracles, expect that the outcomes will happen, but don't be attached to it.

Second, clearly wish that there are no losers. We are brought up to believe that if one person wins, others must lose. We think of life as a zero-sum game. We win, others lose. But that is a mental model and it is possible to think beyond this mental model and consciously intend that all people affected by your actions can benefit.

Realise that your knowledge is limited, your awareness incomplete. So that the actions you take represent one of many ways to achieve your desired outcome.

Finally, step three is to detach and accept. If the outcome that comes your way is different from the one you intended, don't label it good or bad. Embrace it. Cheerfully accept whatever comes your way. This is so contrary to the way in which we normally behave that it may take a lot of practice before you begin experiencing any success with this. I encourage you to keep at it. You will succeed eventually if you gently persist.

Let me introduce the concept of the me-centred universe. You live in a me-centred universe. All of us do. In a me-centred universe, we interpret everything that happens in terms of what's its impact on me. If our spouse gets a great new job, our first reaction is how will this affect our relationship? If our child gets poor grades in school, we think what will the teachers think of me? If our daughter gets tattoos and body piercings, our instinctive feeling is what will my friends think of my parenting? It's all me, me, me, all the way.

There is a quick way for you to check this out. Become the witness and observe your conversations with friends, with colleagues, with clients, with your boss and see how often the words I, me and my come in. If a friend comments about a movie that he has watched, we immediately react by giving our point of view. We are always interjecting 'I' all the time. In a me-centred universe every conversation you have, every thought and outcome to a situation, somehow relates back to 'me'. This translates to stress. We wish to eliminate stress in our lives because we want to lead happier lives. In this, as in all things, we are driven by our self-interest. The paradox is that it is only when we can abandon our self-interest that we can live truly fulfilled lives.

Let us look at self-interest a little more closely. I'd like to explain another universal law that can help you. The law of self-interest states that everybody at all times always acts in his or her perceived self-interest. Even you, especially you. For example, if you're reading this book and paying attention, you're doing so because you expect that it will bring about changes in you that will enable you to lead a happier, more contented existence. Am I saying that everything that you do is driven by self-interest? That is precisely what I am saying and this may come as a shock to some of you. If you're a mother, you may think that you are doing things selflessly for your children, cooking for them, feeding them, taking them to afterschool programme, supervising their homework and so on. You have a model in your head of what a mother should do. By your actions, you are conforming to that model and validating your self-worth. You are doing it for yourself.

Do you contribute to charities and worthy causes? In fact, do you do so anonymously? You have a notion of what an enlightened citizen should do and you're conforming to that model. Everything that you do, everything is in fact done in self-interest. Think about this.

Let's consider an action that you might label completely altruistic. You're driving on a deserted highway, and in front of you there is a car which has a flat tyre. A young mother with children in tow is looking helplessly. You stop. She doesn't have a jack. So, you take yours, lift up the car, replace the tyre with the spare and then travel your way. Have you just performed an altruistic action, yes, you have. But why did you do it? You did it because if you had carried on without helping, you would have felt uncomfortable. You would have thought less about yourself. You would have wondered whether she made it to the next town. You would have wondered how the children fared. By stopping and helping her, you rid yourself of all these anxieties and that's why you did it.

Understanding that everybody at all times always acts in his or her self-interest can help you put down too heavy boulders that you may be carrying, that most people carry at some time or the other. These are the boulders of guilt and blame. Every time you feel guilty about something that you have done, something that you should have done but didn't do, and especially in relationships with others, you're carrying guilt. Recognise that you did what you did, or did not do what you now think you should have done, was because at that time you acted in what you felt was your perceived best interest. Recognise that every time you did what you feel you should not have done or did not do what you now feel you should have done, you were acting at the time in your perceived best self-interest. With the wisdom of hindsight, your notion of self-interest may have changed, but at that time that is what you did. That's a universal law. There is no point in blaming yourself for conforming to the universal law. And so, the guilt drops away. Every time you blame someone, you're being critical of actions that they took in the past or actions that they did not take, that you feel they should have taken. But once again, they did what they did because they were acting in their perceived best self-interest. That's a universal law. They could not do anything different. So, the blame drops away. This law can be very liberating once you fully understand it.

Before we conclude this session, I would like to offer you another homework assignment which will give you a taste of what it might be like to expand beyond your me-centred universe and thereby expand your actions based on self-interest to a higher level.

Get out your journal once more and take notes on this and label the page 'focus on another'. We've talked about how our natural tendency is to relate to our lives in terms of how it affects me. But you can begin to practise how to expand that narrow focus to include others in a genuine way. For the next week, at least once per day and preferably several times a day, focus your attention completely on another person.

Here are some examples on how you can begin doing this. If you're talking with someone, concentrate on what the person is saying. Think of how you can be of service to that person. Notice his or her expression, intonation, body language. Do something every day to make someone's life a little better. Do something to make the world a better place. Do you get annoyed by people who discard plastic drink bottles on the street? Next time, pick up some of those bottles and take them to a recycling bin. Do you get annoyed when people don't flush in the urinals? Flush them as you go past. Are you annoyed when you see cigarette butts on the road? Pick up a couple of them and deposit them in the dustbin. Perhaps you might want to keep napkins with you at all times to enable you to do this.

Consciously look for ways in which you can make the environment and the world better for yourself and everyone else. Here is another challenging way in which you can do this. Every day, make someone's day. Have you ever met someone who inspired and invigorated you in such a fashion that you felt better the whole day, that your well-being was positively impacted? It could be a stranger in a line who cracked jokes that left you exploding in laughter. It could be a waitress who was so attentive that you felt yourself come alive. There are many such occasions you can recall if you set your mind to it. Each of those persons made your day. Return the favour. Every day, think of some way in which you can make someone's day. Some could be known to you like a colleague, a co-worker, a member of your family. Some may be unknown to you like a waiter in the restaurant or your Ola driver. It doesn't matter. What matters is your intent. Make someone's day.

These are difficult things to do and it is probably a good idea to begin slowly and gently. Don't condemn yourself if you can't maintain your focus. Try picking small slots, 10 minutes, 20 minutes, perhaps an hour each day in which you try the exercise. Use your witness. Keep bringing your focus back to the other person. If you find yourself expecting gratitude, note that without judgement and let the desire for gratitude go or refocus on how you can be of service to that person. Remember, you should be grateful to the person because you have the opportunity to be of service. If you find yourself becoming resentful because you did so much and he or she didn't even say thank you, then you are violating the spirit of the exercise. Be practical, but get creative. Remember the law of self-interest. You're doing this exercise for others, but you're actually doing it for yourself. You're not doing it to get a thank you from someone else or to be appreciated. Note your emotional tenor each day and record it in your journal.

5

Finding True Freedom and Happiness

We've talked a lot about how to eliminate the stress in your life by meeting what the universe has to offer you with self-mastery. We have learned how to eliminate or at least reduce stress in our lives. And as we do so, we come closer to finding true freedom and happiness. But first you must gain clarity about what it is that you really want and what makes you truly happy.

What is happiness? It may seem to come fleetingly and go. How can you have the kind of happiness that is unwavering, constant and steady? To understand the answer to this question, you first need to understand your own natural desire for freedom and happiness. These are two interrelated concepts which can help us understand how to find the true happiness that we are seeking.

It is probably accurate to say that everything you do is in some way a quest for happiness in your life. If you're working to get a degree, it's because you perceive that after you attain that degree, you will do something that will make you happier. If you leave your job and accept another, it is because the second job provides you something, perhaps more money, perhaps greater freedom, more authority, but something that will leave you happier. Everything that you do is actually a quest for happiness. But I will venture to state that despite this lifelong quest of yours, you're still not clear on exactly what happiness is.

Let's try an experiment.

Please get out your journal and turn to a fresh page. Carefully read the following question. You will answer it in your journal. What do you need to get in order to be happy? Think about it. What do you need to get in order to be happy? Begin writing.

If you're like most persons, it will not be very long before you have several dozen items on your page. Perhaps you have recorded some of these: Money. Perhaps a great deal of money. A compatible spouse. Good health. Lots of leisure time. The ability to take exotic vacations. Great sex. Children. Some people actually put down the absence of children. Pets. Proficiency in some sport. An invigorating hobby. Good friends. Good relations with your relatives. The list goes on and on. What's on your list? What is it that you feel if I get this, I will be happy. Now get a red marker and draw a line right over your list. I repeat. Draw the line right across and over your list.

I'm going to tell you something that may surprise you. There is nothing you have to get in order to be happy. This is such an important point I want to repeat it. There is nothing you have to get in order to be happy. Think about it. Anything that you can get like great wealth, for example, or fame or fortune, you can un-get, you can lose it. What does this do to your happiness? If your happiness vanishes when you lose what you have gotten, then isn't that a rather frail reed to lean on? Isn't that something too trivial to spend your life seeking?

Your happiness is not dependent on any of the things on your list, although you think that it does. You do not have to do anything to be happy. Happiness is innate in you. It is part of your DNA. It is there. It does not have to be cultivated. It does not have to be created, it does not have to be acquired. It is your birthright.

Many of you will probably find this shocking. A question that I get asked all the time is, 'If happiness is my innate nature, if I am a happy creature by birth, then how come I don't experience it? How come I experience being miserable most of the time?' The answer to that is simple. You have spent your whole life learning to be miserable, learning to be unhappy. And the way you do that is through adopting your mental models. And one of the most powerful mental models that drives your unhappiness is 'if I get this, then I will be happy'. Many of you are living your whole life using this model. I have to get something, so I can do something, so I can be something. If I get a lot of money, I can take exotic vacations and then I will be happy. If I find a beautiful spouse, I can have great sex and then I will be happy. We live our whole lives on this model. Get something, do something, be something. Embedded in that is the notion, if this happens then I will be happy. If I get promoted at work, I will be happy. When my kids grow up and leave for college, I will be happy. When my spouse and I stop fighting, I will be happy. When I am no longer responsible for my parents, I will be happy. It's always in the future. If this happens then I will be happy.

This is a flaw. This is a highly defective, completely dysfunctional model, but you have adopted it so strongly that you don't even question it. Pause for a moment. Think back to sometime in your life when you confronted a scene of spectacular beauty. Perhaps it was a mountain with its peak lost in the clouds. Perhaps it was a heavy snowfall which left the entire land covered in a white carpet. Perhaps it was a rainbow you observed over the ocean. Perhaps it was a wild animal, a tigress cavorting happily with its cubs. It doesn't matter. Can you recall such a scene?

A scene that was so sublime that it took you out of yourself and moved you into a place of immense serenity and peace. Virtually everybody can recall such situations. What happened at that time? You experienced deep peace, did you not? But all of the troubles that plagued you, the financial worries, the relationship troubles, still existed.

What happened at that time is for that instant you accepted the world as it was. You didn't feel that's a wonderful rainbow but it's a little too much on the left side. If I could move it 200 metres to the right, it would be a more perfect scene. You didn't look at the bear and say that's a nice animal but if it was 30 kilos lighter, it would be so much more beautiful. Oh no, the rainbow was perfect where it was, the bear, whatever its size, was perfect. Everything was perfect. In that acceptance, in the knowledge that this was, is, perfect, your wants subdued, at least temporarily. And when your wants were removed from the picture, that happiness, which is a part of you, which has always been a part of you, surfaced and you experienced that peace.

Your life, as it is now, with all of the problems that preoccupy you, that keep you awake at night, your life right now is equally perfect. The problem is not your life. The problem is that you refuse to accept that your life is perfect and, in your refusal to accept it, you experience unhappiness. You have quite literally learned to be unhappy.

Think back to the exercises that we performed in the previous chapter and the concepts you were introduced to – surrender and acceptance. When you surrender to the universe, when you accept whatever outcome is presented to you, then you stop being attached to what you want. You stop thinking 'this is what I need in order to be happy.' And you will find as you practice it that you don't have to seek happiness. Happiness will seek you out and arise unbidden in your heart and your life will blossom.

I'd like to explain another mental model that drives your unhappiness, called frantic doing. Society encourages us to adopt this model. In the model of frantic doing, we are conscious that something in our lives is not as it should be. So, we have to do something about it.

For example, supposing we are unemployed and wish to find a job, the model of frantic doing would have us go to internet career sites and sign up. Prepare several different versions of a résumé. Take aptitude tests to determine which profession, career or job we are best suited for. It would have us send out dozens, hundreds, perhaps thousands of résumés. It would have us contact our friends to see if they know of job openings and if they can set us up with interviews. It would have us call persons to set up informational interviews. It would have us go to career-related events, networking functions, industry trade shows and similar gatherings. We would hit up everyone we know and many we don't and reach out to perfect strangers. And the model goes, if we do enough of this, eventually we will find a job.

Or let's say that we are not in a relationship and would like to be in one. The model of frantic doing would have us sign up for internet dating sites, get our friends to introduce us to potential dates, join social organisations, go to parties, hang out in bars and keep constantly active in this search, and if we do all of this perhaps we will find someone and maybe even get into a relationship.

We generally do not pause to consider whether this frantic effort is actually the best way to achieve what we would like. It frequently turns out that the job we get is unsatisfying, and another dead end. The relationship we enter into is fraught with tension and not very stable.

There is an alternative to the model of frantic doing. This is the model of calm being. In calm being, the witness notes that you are not particularly satisfied with the situation which you are in and would like to be in a different set of circumstances. In calm being you work internally and gain great clarity over what exactly it is that you would like to manifest in your life. And as you gain this utter cold clarity you find that there are generally simpler ways of getting to your goal. This does not mean that you do not need to take action. But you probably need to take much less action and with much less stress than under the model of frantic doing.

One of the students in my programme was about to graduate and he still did not have a job. His classmates, in a similar situation, were frantic with worry. They were desperately sending out résumés badgering the placement department to get them interviews, pestering professors to see if they could place them with companies the professors knew and generally running themselves ragged. My student spent more time on finding clarity about what he wanted to do and with whom. He also made a list of all the skills that he had and the ways in which he could contribute to any company that hired him. He then sat and wrote a very detailed and highly persuasive letter which outlined his strong desire and his unique abilities. He sent this letter to a dozen carefully selected executives, in particular companies. Three of them called him for interviews, and he received two job offers.

Let's move on to the related concept of freedom. What does freedom mean to you? Most persons when they think of freedom, define it as their ability to do whatever they want. They talk in terms of economic freedom, political freedom, freedom of speech, freedom of religion, freedom of the right to assemble, all of them rights are guaranteed in the constitutions of most democracies. But this is freedom defined too narrowly. This is freedom defined as a lack of restriction on our actions.

But think about this, are you truly free? Do you have freedom from the constant desire for more? Think about what a huge proportion of your life is an unending struggle to acquire more things. A bigger house, a more luxurious house, a better car, more belongings of one kind or the other. Do you have addictions of any kind? To drugs, to alcohol, to work, to sex, to watching junk television, to cheap thrillers? Do you overeat? How often do you find yourself unable to pursue a course of action that you know is in your best interest? This, too, is lack of freedom. We don't recognise that this is a lack of freedom. We don't focus on it and therefore we are imprisoned by it. We are imprisoned by our uncontrolled desire, by our lusts, by our inability to do what we recognise in our saner moments is in our best interest. And this lack of freedom contributes immensely to your inability to experience the happiness that is your innate nature.

Pause for a moment to consider what we have just learned. We all have goals. We are all striving for something. To get promoted at work. To have a better relationship with our spouse. To see our children do well in school and college and then in the workplace. We want our offspring to be happily married and productive. We want all of this. Because we sense that this will make us happy. If–then: if this happens, then we will be happy. But if this isn't true, if we don't need any of this to be happy, if happiness is our innate nature, then where does that leave us? What happens to our ambition? What happens to our goals?

I have frequently been asked the question that if the model that I've just outlined to you was adopted, won't it leave one completely passive, unwilling to do anything? If I don't need to do anything to be happy, why should I get out of bed in the morning? I will just lie about all day, watch television, laze around.

Let me tell you a story. Many years ago, there was an Indian sage called Ramakrishna, a fully enlightened being, and he had disciples who were very advanced in their own right. When Ramakrishna died, all his disciples scattered all over India. One of them, later famous as Swami Brahmananda, was on a pilgrimage. He was going towards Benaras when he felt a tremendous weakness overcome him. He had not eaten for days. He lay down under a tree because he was unable to move further, and he believed that his time had come. He was perfectly at peace with this. He lay down and closed his eyes. It was evening and it was chilly. A passer-by saw a holy man lying on the ground and said, oh, he must be feeling cold. And from his belongings, he took a very expensive shawl and covered him up and Swami Brahmananda looked at it and marvelled, 'How wonderful is the universe, I was feeling cold, and he has provided a warm covering.' Even as he was thinking this, another passer-by observed a man perhaps asleep, covered with an inexpensive shawl and quickly gathered it up and went on his way. Swami Brahmananda could not help bursting out laughing. 'How wonderful is the universe! Even as I was thanking it for providing me a warm covering, it removed that covering. Such is the joy of life.'

If you are in that space, if you can truly and completely wholeheartedly accept what is given to you, then yes, it doesn't matter whether you get up in the morning or you don't, you will be happy and fulfilled. But the odds are good that you are not in the same mental space and because you are not, you will be compelled to act, and you will be compelled to act to achieve something. To get that promotion, to have a better relationship with your spouse, to see your children do well.

Recognise this clearly and accept it. There is nothing good or bad about it. It is simply an acknowledgement of where you are.

However, there is one thing that you will give up. You will give up the notion that if you accomplish what you set out to do, then you will be happy. That is the link that is spurious. That is the link which is embedded in your consciousness but which you have to give up. If you give that up, you act because that is what you were put on this earth to do. You will work for your promotion and if you are promoted, wonderful. If you are not promoted, still wonderful. It will not diminish your happiness if you are not promoted. It will not increase your happiness if you are promoted. Your happiness is a constant, complete undertone. So do what you are drawn to do but remember that accomplishing the goal will not necessarily increase your happiness and failure will not diminish it.

As you think about this more and more you will find that in fact it is true. You will find that you do not need to get anything in order to find happiness. There will be more and more occasions in your life when that peace, that serenity, will come unbidden. Celebrate it each time it arrives in your life. But don't particularly mourn it when it goes because it will leave you, and for long periods. You can gently summon it back. You will need patience, endless patience. But if you are gently persistent, you will succeed and then you will find that you are acting. Acting to accomplish something not because it will make you happy, but spontaneously, because this is your path in life. This is what you were called to do.

Visualise this. You wake up in the morning and you're feeling good about yourself. You brush your teeth. You take a shower. The warm water on your body feels invigorating. All of a sudden you feel complete. You feel full. You burst into song. You're not singing to become happy. Your singing is a spontaneous outburst. It comes from your happiness, not as a cause of your happiness.

All of your life can be like that. The actions you take can spring spontaneously from your happiness as opposed to something that you have to do to create happiness. So you move spontaneously through life, doing whatever it is you were set on earth to do and enjoying every minute of it and whatever the outcome of your actions matters not a whit.

Are you beginning to feel comfortable with the notion? That your happiness is not dependent on external circumstances? It is not dependent on your job, on your relationships, on whether or not you have friends in your life, or anything else that you think is so necessary.

Let us explore this issue in a little greater detail.

Here is another visualisation for you. As before, go to a room where you are unlikely to be disturbed, sit with your back straight, your feet flat on the ground or crossed, if that's what you prefer. Close your eyes and take a few deep breaths. Relax. Recall a time in your life when you accomplished something, something big. Perhaps you landed a big customer at work, finished your degree at a prestigious university, or won a competition. Pick any one of these times and recall the details around this event. Connect with your feelings. Did you feel happy? Who was there with you?

Did they say anything to you? How did that make you feel? What was the mental chatter you were experiencing? Were you congratulating yourself on the hard work that you put into the project?

Now, I'd like you to recall a different time in your life, a time when you connected with something bigger than yourself. Do you remember when you were with a group of friends and the conversation flowed freely, and you felt a deep sense of connectedness? Perhaps a similar feeling with family members or witnessing your child being born or simply taking in an amazing sunset. Recall the details around this event and how it felt. Really connect with this feeling of contentment, of fullness. Good.

Take a few deep breaths and open your eyes.

This exercise is a great way to connect with what the Jesuit priest and psychotherapist Antony de Mello calls worldly happiness and soul happiness. Worldly happiness is influenced by the world. It's externally focused, materially focused. It reinforces your individual ego. It requires you to do better than someone else. It fosters your competitive urges. Worldly happiness is fraught with tension because it is predicated on your achieving something and what you can achieve you can also lose. But if you look around, you will find that worldly happiness is what is stressed by your family, friends and co-workers on television, in magazines, and books, in societal values. You're constantly told that you find happiness through these constructs. You find happiness when you win. When you reach the pinnacle of some organisation, your emotional state becomes completely dependent on whether or not you meet the criteria, which are laid down by somebody else. These are worldly criteria. Worldly happiness does not give you peace, does not last, and can easily and quickly be snatched away.

Soul happiness is part of your innate nature. It does not require anything external. You simply have to learn how to let it surface. If soul happiness is so accessible, why aren't we all happy? That's because of the mental models that we have adopted, and by now you have started to see that many of the mental models you use are dysfunctional. They do not serve you well.

To allow true happiness to surface, you require acceptance and non-attachment. We have already discussed how you can learn to accept what is without judgement. Non-attachment is a big concept. You have already begun to see that when you are attached to an outcome, you have more stress and your emotional tenor can lead to a feeling of unhappiness.

What does it truly mean to be non-attached? Think about your witness. The witness notices your circumstances without feeling, like a scientist. This is non-attachment. This is a space that you can reach, but you need to practise. Now that you are beginning to deconstruct your past held ideas about what happiness is, you can be more attuned to what will truly make you happy in your own life.

Here is some homework for you. Take out your journal and take notes on this. Label it, 'What makes me happy?' It is a simple exercise that can help you start connecting with unique aspects in life that bring you true happiness.

For the next month, notice when you are engaged in an activity that makes you come alive. As you notice these activities, write them down. Note what the activity is, how it makes you feel, and what specifically about it is appealing to you. Also, note down things that you do not do but would like to, that you feel drawn to in some way. For example, do you feel drawn to play the guitar, to play squash, or to do mountain climbing? If any activity speaks to you, write it down. After a month, pick any one or two of the activities and begin to cultivate them. Find some way to deepen your experience in it, spending more time, learning more about it. Notice the change in your emotional tenor as you cultivate this aspect of your life. Write it in your journal. Honour the feeling.

It is very important that you perform the activity you have chosen because it calls to you at some deep level. You're not doing it to accomplish anything in a material sense or to demonstrate to someone that you're capable of it. You are just performing it because it feels good. It helps if you break this up into small manageable chunks.

One of my students, a busy investment banker, had always dreamed of being able to play the guitar. Somehow it didn't work out. After taking my course, he determined that he would take action. He decided that he would take small concrete steps each week. For the first step, he found out the names of guitar teachers in his area. The next step, he called up each of them and arranged to take one lesson. For the third step, he picked the teacher with whom he felt most comfortable and signed up for regular lessons. For the fourth step, he purchased a guitar recommended by the teacher he had signed up with. Within a year, he got to the stage where he could play simple tunes on his own, and sometimes he played the guitar simply because he felt like it.

Many centuries ago, when Bodhidharma brought Buddhism to Japan, he spent many months meditating in a cave. Legend has it that his arms atrophied and dropped off. This is commemorated in a Daruma doll. A symbol of happiness, a Daruma doll is weighted at its foundation. So, whenever you knock it over, it bounces back. If you knock it with force, it bounces back equally fast. That is its innate state of being.

True happiness is like a Daruma doll. You can have it. Any time you're knocked down, you can bounce back and the harder you're knocked down, the faster you can bounce back. Keep this in mind as an image, come back to it over and over.

As you become conscious of your own innate happiness and your ability to manifest it at will, I'd like to offer you another universal law that will help you become even more effective. The universe is a force multiplier. It takes whatever you send out, greatly amplifies it and beams it back at you. What is a force multiplier? In military terms, a force multiplier is any device that makes a weapon system far more effective. For example, anti-aircraft batteries are effective against bombers, but anti-aircraft batteries guided by radar, which can lock in on aircraft, are orders of magnitude more effective. The radar guidance system is a force multiplier. It enables you to do far more with fewer resources.

Think of the universe as a giant force multiplier. As I said before, it amplifies what you send out and beams it back at you. You can harness its power and your own creativity by being intentional in your broadcast. Here is how you can do this. As you have already seen, with the law of increase, the practice of gratitude causes those things we appreciate to increase in our lives. You have also seen how you can eliminate stress in your life by not following the mental models that negative emotions can create. What happens when you begin to focus your attention outside of yourself and include others and the greater community?

To help you put this concept into practice, I would like to take you through a guided reflection. So once again, go to a room where you're unlikely to be disturbed. Sit with your back straight, your feet flat on the ground or crossed if you prefer. Take a few deep breaths and relax.

Think about what's right with your work. Most of us spend a good portion of our waking hours at work. Often this is a place where we do not find true peace or happiness. Here is how you can begin to change that dynamic right now. Think about your job. The one that you're in right now. How do you feel about it? What keeps you in this job? Are you happy? Very few persons are passionate about what they do for a living. Many are unhappy. Some are deeply discontented.

Think about a time when you felt frustrated about your job. Notice the two things that are always true every time when you are unhappy or frustrated in your job. First, as you feel frustrated, you're living in a me-centred universe. 'Oh me, poor me. I'm so talented, so bright. Why am I not being recognised? Why am I not being adequately compensated? Why does nobody listen to my ideas? Why do my co-workers not behave as I want them to? Why does my boss not appreciate the contribution I'm making? Oh me, poor me.' We're squarely in a me-centred world when we are unhappy at work.

The second thing that is true is that we are completely ignoring the twenty, thirty or forty things which are actually pretty good about our jobs and focusing completely on the one, two or three things that are bad. More precisely, on the one, two or three things that we think are bad.

Think about this. It will not take you more than a few minutes to recognise the truth of the statement. Every time you're frustrated, angry, unhappy, you're living in a me-centred world and you're completely ignoring the many things that are actually pretty good about your job.

Let's try to shift our perspective. Start thinking about all the components of your job that are actually pretty good. Perhaps most of your co-workers are denizens of hell but there may be a couple who are actually quite good to hang out with. Think about them and feel grateful.

Perhaps most of your customers are horrible but there may be one or two that are actually pleasant to interact with. Think about that. Be grateful for that. Perhaps your boss is a tyrant on most days but there may be some occasions when he actually seems a decent human being. Think about them. Be grateful for them.

Open your eyes and come back to the room. Write down all the things you noted that were actually pretty good about your job. For the time being, just focus on them and note down anything else that reminds you of the rejuvenating, nurturing things about your work.

You've done a great job and I congratulate you for stretching yourself this far. In the next chapter, we're going to take a deeper look into your own personal values and how you can create a life of personal mastery and fulfilment.

6

Create Your Reality

As we move into this final section I'd like to give you some more tools you can use to reach a completely fulfilled life. Let me introduce a final universal law to you. The universe is benevolent. I call this the benevolent universe model. Let me explain.

You probably have the model that the universe is a vast entity that does not know you exist and is indifferent to your wants and needs. Sometimes you might extend this to feel that occasionally the universe wakes up and makes it its business to frustrate you in every way possible. Most of us have some variation of this model. It's not a particularly happy place to be at. How about we try a new mental model. The benevolent universe model. In this model, the universe is a conscious entity. It is aware of you and well disposed towards you. It is all powerful. It organises itself so that it always gives you everything that you need, everything that is good for you, at precisely the moment that you need it. Have you ever seen the Cirque du Soleil performance? There is a huge stage and every section of it is occupied. The aerialist goes up on her bar, leaves it, turns a dizzying array of acrobatics and just as she is about to fall, another bar is there for her to grasp. The universe is exactly like that. It knows what you need and gives it to you at precisely the right time.

Now remember that what you want is not necessarily what is best for you or what you need. Children may want a tub of ice cream, but a wise parent will provide vegetables. When you adopt this model, there are no tragedies in your life. There are no misfortunes. There are only lessons which have been provided to you appropriately, at exactly the correct moment. Pause for a second to consider this model and all its ramifications.

Now let's consider something else. It will be readily obvious to you that even if the model just proposed – the benevolent universe model – was completely false and utter balderdash, if you believed that it was true, your life would be considerably improved. It really doesn't matter whether it is 'true' or 'untrue'. If you believed it was true and acted accordingly, your life would be considerably more bearable, more full of happiness, more full of hope and joy. If the universe is impersonal and indifferent then all the things that happen to you, which you label bad, are random events, so you are at the mercy of unthinking, unknowing, unpredictable forces. This is not a very pleasant universe to live in. But if you believe in the benevolent universe model, there are no tragedies, nothing bad ever happens to you. True, there are some things that you would rather not have happened to you, but you understand that in some way these teach you a lesson and these lessons will lead to greater growth and take you to a place of greater fulfilment and more happiness. And you know this, you know it deeply. And therefore, you do not resent what other persons might term tragedies. You learn from them, and you move on. This is a considerably more inspiring and joyous place to live in.

So when we talked about surrender in a previous chapter, we surrender to a force more powerful, more knowledgeable than us. I am now suggesting that we surrender to the benevolent universe, which is not only more powerful, not only more knowledgeable, but thoroughly well disposed towards us. Like a fond parent, it arranges itself so that it brings all manner of good things into our life. It does not allow us to confront anything which in any way would impede our growth or harm us. Nothing that happens to us can possibly be bad.

The problem is that even if we intellectually recognise that this model is a far better one for us to adopt than the one we presently use, this doesn't mean that we can adopt it. We cannot force ourselves to believe something, but we can allow that belief to arise in us. Would you like to believe in the benevolent universe model?

Here is some homework for you. Once again get your journal. Open it to a fresh page and put down the heading 'The Benevolent Universe'. Go back over your life and think of a situation which you labelled bad. At the time, you were convinced that this was an unmitigated disaster. Perhaps you now have a slightly different perspective, or perhaps you still think of it as bad. Recall it to mind and then play around with the possibility that it was good.

Quite possibly you will not be able to accept that it was completely good but be open to the possibility that there were good aspects to it. See how these play out.

One of my students was carrying a heavy baggage of guilt over the death of his son. His son died in a tragic accident while quite young. When he tried this exercise, he was immediately able to recognise that as a result of this tragedy, he had an unusual ability to empathize with others who were coping with personal tragedies. In his off hours, he was a counsellor and extraordinarily effective in helping families come to terms with their loss and move on with life. He can now readily accept that his own personal tragedy enabled him to grow and be more effective in helping others.

Now think of your life and all the situations that you are confronting. Mentally, you've already labelled some of them as good, some of them as bad, and some of them as neutral. Throw this basket aside. Think of everything that has happened, is happening, will happen in your life as good. Embrace each and every event and outcome and then move forward from there. If you still find it too difficult, don't beat yourself up. Keep copious notes in your journal. Each time you confront something which you would have labelled as bad, put a question mark instead of the label 'bad' and then see the ways in which it is actually beneficial to you and is helping you grow. Do this also with the major events in your past. See how they helped you grow. See how they cumulatively brought you to the place where you are today. See how these events engendered a spiritual awakening in you. Let all of this seep in.

As you continue doing this exercise, spend some time each day thinking about the possibility that the universe is benevolent. Every time you experience one of the miracles we talked about in an earlier chapter, note it down. Idly play with the notion that perhaps this was the universe reaching out for your benefit to make life better for you. As you continue doing this and as the number of entries you make in your journal grows, you will come to a tipping point. Either you have to accept that you have been on the beneficiary side of an incredible number of random occurrences, all of which helped you, or you accept the possibility that maybe, just maybe, the universe is benevolent, is sentient and is reaching out to you and trying to help you. When you reach this tipping point, redouble your efforts. Look for more evidence that the universe is a sentient being working with you, for you, through you and helping you at every stage. And as you look for it, you will find more such evidence and as you find more such evidence, your belief becomes stronger and as your belief becomes stronger, you will find more evidence and soon you will find yourself becoming embedded in the notion of a benevolent universe.

As you are working with the benevolent universe model, some of you may be thrown off by senseless tragedies. Some of these are impersonal earthquakes, tsunamis, volcanic eruptions. Some of these are man-made – genocide, war, disease. How can you fit all of these into a benevolent universe model? They do fit, but before you can make sense of this, it is important that you work with the benevolent universe model in your own situation, come to terms with it and recognise that that is how it is operating in your life. It is only when you have succeeded in doing so that you will gain a perspective that will include the tragedies that surround us.

Consider a forest fire. It can devour hundreds, thousands of acres of trees. Countless animals are burnt. A lot of suffering ensues. But we now know that forest fires are a necessary part of an ecological balance. Forest fire gets rid of undergrowth, clears ground, opens up the canopy to greater sunlight and enriches soil with ash from previous generations of plant. It is a continual cycle of destruction and rebirth. In exactly the same way in a fashion that we cannot fully understand or fathom, the tragedies that we see around us have inherent in them the seed of something that eventually will sprout and be for the good of all humanity. This is something that we sense, and we feel, not necessarily something we can intellectually understand. Wait for such a feeling to emerge in you.

There are many ways in which the model of a benevolent universe can help you. For example, the notion of networking. Many persons, perhaps most persons, do not feel comfortable networking. There is a reason for that. As traditionally understood, networking consists of figuring out who could potentially be of help to you and coming up with a way of ingratiating yourself to that person. It is self-serving and at some level, many of us feel uncomfortable with this idea. In fact, the very notion of networking or forming or creating a network is self-serving. Think about it. You want to get to know someone because somehow you perceive that there is a benefit to you in this.

Let me suggest an alternative, a method of forming very deep, long-lasting relationships with a group of persons who will actively work to further your own interests. You can form such a network without ever doing anything that makes you feel uncomfortable. Here is how you begin.

First, recognise that the best way to form a network is not to try. Don't try to build a network. Don't try to create a network. Don't try to form a network. Instead allow a network to form around you. Here is how you do this. There are many times in life where you come across a person who's doing something that moves you deeply, that inspires you. Perhaps it's an executive in your company who has come up with a unique method for empowering her workers. Perhaps it's a colleague who spends his time coaching at-risk children. Perhaps it's someone you read about who has tackled some social problem with great success. There are many occasions when we feel inspired by such stories. What we typically do when this happens is we feel good, we feel good about ourselves, we feel good about the world and about our role in it and then life encroaches, and we move on. That is a mistake. Don't do it.

Here is what I recommend. Every time you get a glow of satisfaction, a warm feeling when you read about someone who's doing something that you admire, record it in your journal. If you do this consistently for a couple of months, you will have anywhere from six to two dozen incidents. At the end of this period go back to these entries and determine which people continue to inspire you at a deep level. Reach out to the person with the sincere note expressing admiration for what he or she is doing, mentioning how you have been inspired and offer to help. It is nice if you can come up with a specific offer indicating what you're willing to do. Of course, you have to be fully prepared to deliver on the help if you're called upon. The only reason you make this offer is because if it is accepted and you do what you said you would, you will help make the world a better place, and this makes you feel good. If you do this regularly you will be amazed at how many times your offer is in fact accepted and how deep relationships form effortlessly as a consequence. If you do this consistently for two years, you will find that you don't have to create a network, a very deep network; of people aligned with your values has sprung up around you. The benevolent universe has created this for you.

A leading executive coach with dozens of CEO clients was reminiscing about his early days. He was not well known and was struggling to find clients. Nevertheless he contributed free workshops and pro bono coaching sessions to several non-profits. The director of one of the non-profits introduced him to a member of the board who was the CEO of a large consulting firm. That CEO became his client and introduced him to many other CEOs who also became clients.

Look at your own situation. Which is the organisation or individual that moves and inspires you? What can you do to make them more effective? What can you contribute – your time, money, talent or creativity? The benevolent universe model can help us in many areas of life. For example, take your job. If you are like most people, you are frequently discontented and unhappy doing what you do. This misery comes because you are relentlessly focused on what you want to happen. You want the universe to unfold in the manner that you desire. While you are concentrating on the ways in which your desires are not being met, you are ignoring the many ways in which your other desires are being satisfied.

Time after time, I have come across persons who feel that there is an ideal job somewhere out there, and it is their task to find it. Invariably, they define their ideal job in terms of a set of parameters, all of them external. This is how much it pays. This is the type of person their boss is. These are the skills that they use. This is the amount of travel that they do. Here are the kinds of colleagues they have and on and on and on. Perhaps you do the same. It is important for you to realise that this exact set of circumstances does not exist. But even if it did exist, and if you were plugged into it, it would not take very long, certainly less than six months, before you were equally miserable in it.

It is very important for you to recognise and realise that passion does not exist in the job. Passion exists inside you and if you do not learn to ignite it within yourself right where you are at this instant, you will never find it outside. Let me repeat that.

Passion exists inside you, not inside the job, and the way you create your ideal job is by first igniting the passion within you and the place to begin is right where you are at this instant.

Here is how you can go about this. Once again get out your journal and turn to a fresh page. Label it 'ideal job' and start recording all of the things in your job that are actually pretty good. Do you get a salary? Even an inadequate one. Be grateful for it. That is the salary that enables you to go out for dinner, take in an occasional movie and do all of the things that you find pleasurable. Is your boss a tyrant? But perhaps there are some days when he actually behaves like a decent human being. Be grateful for that. Perhaps your customers or clients are disagreeable, but maybe there is one who is actually quite fun to deal with. Be grateful for that. Be grateful for small things like the restrooms are clean and the drinks in the vending machine are cold. Be grateful for big things such as the opportunity to learn things that you otherwise would never have. As you make such a list, you will be amazed to discover how many things there are in your present job that are actually quite good. Pause and feel grateful for each and every one of them. As you did in the appreciation and gratitude exercise, you will let a feeling envelop you and flow out from you. Remember, you're also invoking the law of increase.

As a next step, pick any one area which is important to you and decide that you're going to undertake a project to increase its space in your life. For example, if a particular customer is fun to work with, you may decide that you're going to acquire more customers like this one or perhaps you decide that you want to transform all your customer relationships into something similar. It's entirely your call. For the next month, you're going to do something every day that will help bring this about. It is very important that whatever tasks you undertake involve significant learning on your part. You have to push beyond your comfort horizon. Do something every day to bring this into being. At the end of the month, evaluate where you are. If you find that you have not yet completed your project, give yourself more time. If you do this for a year, you will have completed four to eight projects, each one of which would have increased some component of your job that you really like, that brings you alive, that makes you fulfilled. And as you do this, you will find that your job has changed completely. The benevolent universe will arrange to take you a long way towards your ideal job.

As you become more comfortable with the notion of a benevolent universe, you will find that it provides you many things. It will provide you a network of deep relationships with a group of persons who will actively work to further your own interests. It will provide you the opportunity to find your ideal job, one which makes you come alive, which invigorates you. In fact, the benevolent universe can even provide you with your ideal life.

Here is a guided visualisation practice that you can begin. As before, go to a room where you are not likely to be disturbed, sit in a comfortable chair with your back straight and your feet on the ground. It is okay to sit cross-legged if you prefer. Close your eyes, take a few deep breaths. Feel yourself relaxing.

We're going to visit your ideal day. You're going to be playful and come up with a vision of what you would like your life to be. In your ideal life, what is a typical day? You wake up in the morning. Where are you? Are you alone, or is there someone with you? How do you feel? Where do you live? What are your surroundings like? What would you want your surroundings to be like? Are you close to the ocean? Can you see the mountains? Are there trees around you? Can you hear the birds chirping? Who do you see around you? Are you married? Do you have a partner? Do you have children? How do you feel about them? How would you like them to feel about you?

Imagine yourself getting dressed. What do you wear? Do you wear a suit or formal clothes or do you dress in comfortable, informal clothing? How do you get to work? Do you take a bus or a subway or public transportation? Do you drive? Do you walk? What do you do? What kind of organisation are you a part of or are you an entrepreneur who has formed his or her own organisation? How does what you do benefit you? How does it benefit others? How does it benefit the world at large? What kind of feelings emerge in you as you work? Do they change through the day? What happens after work? Do you have any hobbies? What are they and how do you feel about them? What do you do at the end of the day? Do you relax with a drink? Do you watch television? Do you workout? Do you simply lie back and listen soothing music? What would you like your life to be? Play around with different scenarios and pick the one that calls to you. Imagine that you are in fact living such a life. Be gentle with yourself. No force. Just imagination and playfulness.

Take a few deep breaths and open your eyes. Come back gently to the present moment. It is important that you repeat this practice as often as you can. In every case, it should be fun. It should be playful. If ever you feel a sense of stress, if ever feelings arise, 'I am never going to get there. This is all fixed and make-believe,' stop immediately. But you will find that if you can consistently play with this idea, modify it, have fun doing it, then the benevolent universe will gradually in bits and pieces start manifesting it in your life.

Epilogue

We have covered a lot of ground in this book. We have learned about mental chatter. And how we can prevent its destructive effects and harness its creative potential. We have learned about mental models and how we use them to construct our reality, a reality that we then proceed to experience. We have learned how to deconstruct parts of our reality that we don't like and to create alternative realities that are much better. We have learned how to use the witness to reduce or even eliminate stress. We have learned about the me-centred universe and its corrosive influence, and we have also learned how to expand our awareness to include others and eventually all of creation.

We have understood what happiness and freedom really mean, and we have learned how to use universal laws to increase happiness and freedom in our lives. We have learned about the law of increase, which states that whatever we appreciate and are truly thankful for will increase in our life. We have learned about the law of self-interest which states that everybody at all times always acts in his or her perceived self-interest, everybody, even you, especially you, but when we understand the law of self-interest, we can use it to eliminate the boulders of blame and guilt which we have been carrying all our lives. We have learned about the benevolent universe, and we have learned to acknowledge it and as we do so it acts as a force multiplier and brings in all kinds of good things into our lives.

Perhaps you've already seen significant change happen in your life. Congratulations! The exercises, the assignments, the visualisations in this book are tools. These are the tools that you will use to make your life even better. Continue using them because they become more powerful as you gain experience. As you use these tools constantly, you will find that they combine to ignite a passion within you, a passion for your job, a passion for life itself.

Before we conclude, I'd like to share a story with you. A story that illustrates many of the points we have discussed. There was a king in ancient times who had a very able and enlightened minister. This minister was a person of the highest integrity and greatest wisdom. He genuinely cared for the subjects and was responsible for enacting laws which greatly increased the prosperity of the country. He was very beloved, he was a judge, he was a lawmaker, he was an inspiring figure. The king relied on him for the daily administration of his kingdom. One day, while taking his morning constitutional, the minister heard a rustling in some bushes close by. He investigated and came across seven jars of gold coins. Six of the jars were completely full of gold coins, but the seventh was only about three-quarters full. Amazed at his good fortune, he had all the jars taken to his house and locked them in his safe. As he contemplated his sudden wealth, he felt some slight discontentment. It is unfortunate that the seventh jar is not full, he found himself thinking. Let me fill it up. He sold some of his property, converted it into gold coins and put it in the seventh jar. To his amazement, it did not fill up. He sold more of his property and acquired more gold coins. He put them all in the seventh jar, but it still remained three-quarter full. Gradually he became obsessed. He liquidated all of his holdings, converted into gold coins, but still the seventh jar remained three-quarter full. He asked his wife for her jewellery, sold it, converted that into gold coins and still it did not become full. By now it had become a full-blown obsession with him. He discharged all the servants in his household, took the money saved, put it into the seventh jar and still it was not full. He sold all his worldly goods, his wife's clothes, heirlooms he received from his father, his prayer vessels, even the formal clothes that came to him in his role as minister. He cut down on the number of meals in his household. He became emaciated but still the jar did not become full. He discharged his son's tutor and used the money he saved from it to fill the seventh jar and still it was not full.

The king observed a change in his minister. He was no longer as diligent in the performance of his duties. He seemed to be weak and sickly. One day, he summoned the minister and sat him down. 'Tell me what is happening with you, what are these changes I have observed,' he demanded. The minister remained silent. The king noticed that his clothing was threadbare and asked him why he no longer wore his royal gown. The minister was silent. A sudden flash of intuition struck the king. 'Did you find the seven jars of gold?' he demanded. The minister was taken aback. 'How did you know?' he asked. The king laughed. 'I had them buried in the deepest forests so that nobody would come across them,' he said. 'However did you find them?' The minister explained the circumstances under which he discovered them. The king laughed again. 'Doubtless this is the work of some demon who wanted to undermine my kingdom,' he said. 'Don't you know? You can never fill the seventh jar no matter how hard you try by putting more gold into it.' The minister was astonished. 'How do you know so much about it? Please tell me how can I fill the seventh jar.'

The king laid his arm around the minister's shoulders and said, 'So many people have been ruined by the seven jars. There is only one way in which you can fill the seventh jar. Do you want to know what that is?' 'Yes, yes,' said the minister eagerly. 'Here is what you do,' the king counselled. 'Take the seventh jar, the one which is empty, and lock it up in your strongbox. Don't go near it. Take the six jars which are full and start spending freely from them. Give them away to charity. Do things with them but here is a proviso – do things with them which will only bring good to a large segment of the population. It is very important that you use the gold to bring good to a larger community.' 'But I want to have all the jars of gold full. How will this help?' demanded the minister. 'Don't ask questions,' retorted the king. 'Just do as I say.'

So, with great doubt, the minister went his way. He locked up the seventh jar of gold in his strongroom. He called his wife and asked her to buy jewellery and fine clothes. He asked her to hire all the servants that they had discharged and to bring back the tutor for his son. The minister started spending on projects that he had always wished to bring into being but did not have the wherewithal to before. He gave alms freely.

He built dams for irrigation projects. He built housing for the poor, for the itinerant. He made sure that there were rest houses for travellers, and as he did all this, he found something amazing. No matter how much he spent from the six full jars of gold, they remained full. 'How could this be,' he wondered. 'Let me see what has happened to the seventh jar.' And he opened his strong room and found that the seventh jar had also become full.

That is how life works. If you focus on the empty jar, if you focus on what is missing in your life, you will never succeed, but if you concentrate on the good things of your life and spend from there, you will find that the lack you experience in your life disappears. Your seventh jar will become full as well.

That is my sincere wish for you as you travel on this journey of life – that your seventh jar also becomes full and it will become full if you concentrate on spending from the jars, the jars of all of the good things that are already a part of your life. Focus on them, celebrate them, be grateful for them, and as you do, the things which will make your life full will mysteriously appear, and you will lead a life of such fullness as you cannot even comprehend or conceive of today.

Acknowledgements

This book would not have come about if certain individuals had not conspired to make it happen or simply given me the energy I needed to cross the finish line.

My wife, Meena, who managed our house and gave me time to write.

My daughter, Gowri, and son-in-law, Abhinav, who encouraged me to keep going when I was ready to stop and call it a day.

My son, Gautam, who was always ready to play chess with me when I needed a break. Some day I will give him a tough game. And his wife, Anisha, who exemplifies hard work.

My grandchildren – Krish, Nyra and Kyra – who are bundles of joy and the epitome of boundless energy.

Jacqueline Fox, my right-hand person, who arranged my coaching calls and other engagements in a manner that gave me gobs of free time.

Mekhala Moorthy, who sought me out and gently prodded me and worked with me and has faith that many will benefit from the ideas shared here.

And last but not least, the thousands of people who have taken my course, attended my talks and workshops and written me uplifting notes from all over the world. Bless you and may you progress rapidly on your own journey to everlasting joy.

Index

About the Author

Srikumar Rao is an elite coach who works with a select group of entrepreneurs, professionals and senior executives who are already successful and are now ready to make a dent in the universe. They recognise that life is a spiritual journey and wish to imbue that understanding into every facet of their lives.

He holds a PhD from Columbia Business School, and his courses have been among the most popular and highest rated at many of the world's top business schools. His work has been covered extensively by major media worldwide. He is the author of *Are You Ready to Succeed?: Unconventional Strategies for Achieving Personal Mastery in Business and Life*, *Happiness at Work: Be Resilient, Motivated, and Successful—No Matter What* and *Modern Wisdom, Ancient Roots: The Movers and Shakers' Guide to Unstoppable Success.* He is also the creator and narrator of the audio learning course.

Millions of people have listened to Rao's TED Talk and other recordings and attended his programmes and workshops. He leads you into a rabbit hole, and you determine how far you want to go. You may wish to travel only a short distance and settle for a life in which you are much more successful, have better relationships and enjoy more peace; or you may wish to go all the way and reach what sages have called by many names – enlightenment, Nirvana and awakening. Be aware that if you get *there*, there will be no *you* left to celebrate this.

Rao's approach is effective because he draws from the world's greatest masters. They understood human dilemmas and came up with solutions that have been tested over millennia and proven to work. He is unique in his ability to convert these powerful teachings into exercises acceptable to intelligent people in a post-industrial society. This has led clients to seek his sage counsel on both personal and professional matters. Coaching with Srikumar Rao will make you exponentially more successful if you are diligent in your practice.

Learn more about his work at https://theraoinstitute.com.

You can reach him at srikumar.rao@theraoinstitute.com.